Hardy Country

Late spring in the Frome Valley. This is a
landscape that I find quite irresistible because of
the lushness of the vegetation. A lot of the
meadows have still not been 'improved' too much
and you can still find a good variety of grasses,
wild flowers and stinging nettles. Later in the
summer, there are large numbers of Small
Tortoiseshells which have fed as caterpillars on
the nettles.

HARDY COUNTRY

Gordon Beningfield

Introduction and captions by
GORDON BENINGFIELD

Text by
ANTHEA ZEMAN

ALLEN LANE

ALLEN LANE
Penguin Books Ltd
536 King's Road
London SW10 OUH

First published 1983

Edited by Ian Cameron and Jill Hollis
Designed by Ian Cameron
Produced by Cameron Books Ltd
2a Roman Way, London N7 8XG

Set in Linotype Times
Printed in Holland by Royal Smeets Offset, Weert

British Library Cataloguing in Publication Data

Beningfield, Gordon
    Hardy Country
    1. Dorset—Description and travel
    I. Title
    914.23'304857   DA670.D7

ISBN 0-7139-1451-3

Gordon Beningfield wishes to thank everyone who has helped
him in Dorset, particularly Peter, Stella and Cheryl Ford.

CONTENTS

PICTURES

…This yearly gathering was upon the summit of a hill which retained in good preservation the remains of an ancient earthwork, consisting of a huge rampart and entrenchment of an oval form encircling the top of the hill, though somewhat broken down here and there. To each of the two chief openings on opposite sides a winding road ascended, and the level green space of twenty or thirty acres enclosed by the bank was the site of the fair. A few permanent erections dotted the spot, but the majority of visitors patronized canvas alone for resting and feeding under during the time of their sojourn here.

Shepherds who attended with their flocks from long distances started from home two or three days, or even a week, before the fair, driving their charges a few miles each day—not more than ten or twelve—and resting them at night in hired fields by the wayside at previously chosen points, where they fed, having fasted since morning. The shepherd of each flock marched behind, a bundle containing his kit for the week strapped upon his shoulders, and in his hand his crook, which he used as the staff of his pilgrimage. Several of the sheep would get worn and lame, and occasionally a lambing occurred on the road. To meet these contingencies, there was frequently provided, to accompany the flocks from the remoter points, a pony and waggon into which the weakly ones were taken for the remainder of the journey…

When the autumn sun slanted over Greenhill this morning and lighted the dewy flat upon its crest, nebulous clouds of dust were to be seen floating between the pairs of hedges which streaked the wide prospect around in all directions. These gradually converged upon the base of the hill, and the flocks became individually visible, climbing the serpentine ways which led to the top. Thus, in a slow procession, they entered the opening to which the roads tended, multitude after multitude, horned and hornless—blue flocks and red flocks, buff flocks and brown flocks, even green and salmon-tinted flocks, according to the fancy of the colourist and the custom of the farm. Men were shouting, dogs were barking, with greatest animation, but the thronging travellers in so long a journey had grown nearly indifferent to such terrors, though they still bleated piteously at the unwontedness of their experiences, a tall shepherd rising here and there in the midst of them, like a gigantic idol amid a crowd of prostrate devotees.

The great mass of sheep in the fair consisted of South Downs and the old Wessex horned breeds; to the latter class Bathsheba's and Farmer Boldwood's mainly belonged. These filed in about nine o'clock, their vermiculated horns lopping gracefully on each side of their cheeks in geometrically perfect spirals, a small pink and white ear nestling under each horn. Before and behind came other varieties, perfect leopards as to the full rich substance of their coats, and only lacking the spots. There were also a few of the Oxfordshire breed, whose wool was beginning to curl like a child's flaxen hair, though surpassed in this respect by the effeminate Leicesters, which were in turn less curly than the Cotswolds. But the most picturesque by far was a small flock of Exmoors, which chanced to be there this year. Their pied faces and legs, dark and heavy horns, tresses of wool hanging round their swarthy foreheads, quite relieved the monotony of the flocks in that quarter.

All these bleating, panting, and weary thousands had entered and were penned before the morning had far advanced, the dog belonging to each flock being tied to the corner of the pen containing it. Alleys for pedestrians intersected the pens, which soon became crowded with buyers and sellers from far and near.

In another part of the hill an altogether different scene began to force itself upon the eye towards mid-day. A circular tent, of exceptional newness and size, was in course of erection here. As the day drew on, the flocks began to change hands, lightening the shepherds' responsibilities, and they turned their attention to this tent and inquired of a man at work there, whose soul seemed concentrated on tying a bothering knot in no time, what was going on.

'The Royal Hippodrome Performance of Turpin's Ride to York and the Death of Black Bess,' replied the man promptly, without turning his eyes or leaving off tying.

As soon as the tent was completed the band struck up highly stimulating harmonies, and the announcement was publicly made, Black Bess standing in a conspicuous position on the outside, as a living proof, if proof were wanted, of the truth of the oracular utterances from the stage over which the people were to enter…

from *Far from the Madding Crowd*.

INTRODUCTION

It is now fourteen years since I started to visit Dorset. I first became interested in Hardy and his vision of the English countryside through reading a magazine article about him. It didn't take more than a look at one or two poems and a novel to make me realise that I wanted to go to Dorset with the idea of tracking down anything that might be left of the countryside that had so obviously influenced Hardy all his life.

My first visit to Dorset was even more rewarding than I could have expected, because, without having to search very far, I was able to find what I was looking for. There are still tiny fragments of Dorset that remain unchanged—if you go to the right places, not necessarily ones that can be identified exactly with those in the novels, you can almost hear Hardy speaking to you in the countryside, the wildlife and the people.

Since that first visit, I have been going back regularly in search of Hardy. Each year, I first visit the county in spring, say in May, and immediately have the feeling that I had as a child of being engulfed by the countryside, of having my own special place where nobody can find me. Every time, when I first turn off the main road into the leafy lanes, I unfailingly have a sort of lost feeling of vanishing into the landscape. Perhaps it is because of this sense of excitement that I have chosen to keep visiting Dorset rather than to live there. I am afraid that by actually living in Dorset I would lose this magic that is partly in my imagination but is also backed up by my personal experience of rediscovering the places each spring.

I do not want to suggest that Dorset as a whole still looks as it did in Hardy's day or even as it is presented in this book—although I have painted only what I have seen, I have obviously selected the landscapes and details that appealed to me. The county has suffered terribly from forestry and farming. Heathland, which was such an important element in the landscape of Dorset and consequently in Hardy's novels, has largely been ploughed up or turned into lifeless forests of Christmas trees by the Forestry Commission. When you look behind Hardy's birthplace in Higher Bockhampton hoping to see the heathland that was the inspiration for Egdon Heath in the novels, you see nothing but dreary rows of conifers. I have been agitating to have them clear-felled in the hope that the heathland plants will begin to grow back again.

You have to search now for unspoiled downland with its soft turf cropped by generations of sheep and rabbits, a rich and stable environment with its own flowers and its own butterflies. Instead, there are great swathes of ploughed land used for large-scale cereal growing, reducing everything to the same hedgeless, flowerless monotony. I would not want anyone to be complacent about the parts of Dorset that have so far escaped this fate. The inadequacy of our conservation laws is such that in 1980 a third of the sites in Dorset designated as being of special scientific interest were damaged in a single year. Against this background, it is obvious that nothing in Dorset is safe.

Heathland is a very strong element in Hardy's novels, particularly in *The Return of the Native*. This is a piece of heathland near Corfe Castle. I thought of Hardy's description near the beginning of *The Return of the Native*: 'Before him stretched the long, laborious road, dry, empty, and white. It was quite open to the heath on each side, and bisected that vast dark surface like the parting-line on a head of black hair, diminishing and bending away on the furthest horizon.' When I started to paint the picture, I decided that the track needed someone walking along it and thought why not me? After all, I had walked across there late in the day. And so I put myself in.

Left:
Red campion, a flower that is characteristic of Dorset in the spring.

Luckily, there are parts of Dorset with little valleys and steep-sided coombes that are difficult to farm in this way, where the thickets and big hedgerows and old meadows remain. Here the small family farms still survive and operate very much as they have always done, with the sons and daughters working on the farm and the farmer's wife going out to feed the chickens. Often, of course, the farmer's son goes off to college and never returns to the life of a simple farmer but becomes something rather more grand.

I found one superb small family farm near Corfe Castle, with a wonderful view across to the castle itself. It had geese and chickens running around all over the farmyard and a bedstead leaning up against the barn. There were even cows with horns. The life style of farmers like this constantly throws up images that seem to be straight out of Hardy.

Sheep resting out of the midday sun in the shade of a clump of oak trees. I found this scene near Shaftesbury.

I was very lucky to find in the Marshwood Vale a family that still uses binders at harvest time and stooks the corn. Each November, they drag out their old thrashing machine to thrash it. Apart from being visually superb, this was a happy occasion, with the four or five men who were working there breaking off from time to time to laugh and joke and chase rats and mice with their Jack Russell terrier. There are quite a few farms in Dorset that are still using binders and thrashing machines, objects that are so ancient that the farms have to do their own running repairs and buy any old machines that they can find to use as a source of spares. The traditional methods of harvesting are kept up, not in any spirit of nostalgia or stubbornness, but for the good reason that the farms grow long-stalked corn and the thrashing machine leaves them with long straw that they then supply to a thatcher.

An old binder which is still used on a farm in the Marshwood Vale. I remember binders being used in Hertfordshire in my school days, but you never see them now except in out-of-the-way places like this.

The Dorset coastline between Lulworth Cove and Kimmeridge Bay. It is my favourite coastline because the soft, green downland reaches right to the edge of the cliffs themselves. I am not at all fond of the sea, but from this vantage point I greatly enjoy the Dorset coast.

Right:
A spring that comes out of a wall in a village in the Marshwood Vale. At some time, it has been capped with a stone lion's head, and hanging down on a chain is a bell-shaped bronze drinking cup. A later addition that I did not paint is a sign saying that the water is not fit for drinking.

The farmers were not the only people who reminded me of Hardy. When I was wandering around Dorset, I came upon a group of gipsies who went around in horse-drawn vehicles and seemed to have been plucked straight out of the last century. I have met other fascinating people through contacts or amazing strokes of luck. Visiting my mother in Hertfordshire, I met one of her friends who told me that she knew a hurdle-maker, and it then emerged that he lived in Dorset. To find a hurdle-maker today still working in the woods, making sheep hurdles, is quite extraordinary, particularly when the wood is carpeted with bluebells and there are nightingales singing. Needless to say, he is a happy man, who loves his work.

Some of the people I have met in Dorset seem to have stepped straight out from the pages of Hardy. Many of them could find a place in the novels, especially in those founded on Hardy's deep knowledge of the countryside and rural life. Dorset and its people draw me into the world of Tess the milkmaid in *Tess of the D'Urbervilles* and of Gabriel Oak the shepherd in *Far from the Madding Crowd*. The cows of the Frome Valley today may be the inevitable Friesians, but the watermeadows in the early morning still recall Tess and Angel Clare:

'At these non-human hours they could get quite close to the waterfowl. Herons came, with a great bold noise as of opening doors and shutters, out of the boughs of a plantation which they frequented at the side of the mead; or, if already on the spot, hardily maintained their standing in the water as the pair walked by, watching them by moving their heads round in a slow, horizontal, passionless wheel, like the turn of puppets by clockwork.

'They could then see the faint summer fogs in layers, woolly, level, and apparently no thicker than counterpanes, spread about the meadows in detached remnants of small extent. On the gray moisture of the grass were marks where the cows had lain through the night—dark-green islands of dry herbage the size of their carcases, in the general sea of dew. From each island proceeded a serpentine trail, by which the cow had rambled away to feed after getting up, at the end of which trail they found her; the snoring puff from her nostrils, when she recognized them, making an intenser little fog of her own amid the prevailing one.

'Or perhaps the summer fog was more general, and the meadows lay like a white sea, out of which the scattered trees rose like dangerous rocks. Birds would soar through it into the upper radiance, and hang on the wing sunning themselves, or alight on the wet rails subdividing the mead, which now shone like glass rods. Minute diamonds of moisture from the mist hung, too, upon Tess's eylashes, and drops upon her hair, like seed pearls...'

The sheep on the downland will probably not be Dorset Horns, but the scene still echoes the world of Gabriel Oak. It is not too difficult to find today an equivalent of Hardy's description of 'midnight on the eve of St. Thomas's, the shortest day in the year':

'Norcombe Hill—not far from lonely Toller-Down—was one of the spots which suggest to a passer-by that he is in the presence of a shape approaching the indestructible as nearly as any to be found on earth. It was a featureless convexity of chalk and soil—an ordinary specimen of those smoothly-outlined protuberances of the globe which may remain undisturbed on some great day of confusion, when far grander heights and dizzy granite precipices topple down.

'The hill was covered on its northern side by an ancient and decaying plantation of beeches, whose upper verge formed a line over the crest, fringing its arched curve against the sky, like a mane. To-night these trees sheltered the southern slope from the keenest blasts, which smote the wood and floundered through it with a sound as of grumbling, or gushed over its crowning boughs in a weakened moan. The dry leaves in the ditch simmered and boiled in the same breezes, a tongue of air occasionally ferreting out a few, and sending them spinning across the grass. A group or two of the latest in date amongst this dead multitude had remained till this very mid-winter time on the twigs which bore them, and in falling rattled against the trunks with smart taps.

'Between this half-wooded, half-naked hill, and the vague, still horizon that its summit indistinctly commanded, was a mysterious sheet of fathomless shade—the sounds from which suggested that what it concealed bore some humble resemblance to features here. The thin grasses, more or less coating the hill, were touched by the wind in breezes of differing powers, and almost of differing natures—one rubbing the blades heavily, another raking them piercingly, another brushing them like a soft broom. The instinctive act of human-kind was to stand and listen, and learn how the trees on the right and the trees on the left wailed or chaunted to each other in the regular antiphonies of a cathedral choir; how hedges and other shapes to leeward then caught the note, lowering it to the tenderest sob; and how the hurrying gust then plunged into the south, to be heard no more.'

It is the completeness of Hardy's view of the countryside that excites me. In novels like *Tess of the D'Urbervilles*, the landscape is not just a backdrop to the action, but is a living place out of which everything grows. And everything in it is significant—not just the geography, but the people with their ways of life and their traditions, the wildlife, the time of day or year and the weather. Perhaps the importance of the setting as the starting point of the books is best expressed in the magnificent opening of *The Return of the Native* with its portrait of Egdon Heath. Only isolated fragments may now remain of Dorset heathland, but you can still find it here and there, for example in the part of Winfrith Heath that is not covered by the Nuclear Research Station and can be seen from the railway on the way to Dorchester. In fact, the various areas

Corfe Castle is a recognisable Hardy location. I stayed there for almost a day in May wondering how to paint it. Later, I went back inland to look at an old farm from which I saw the rather misty silhouette of the castle in the distance with the typical Dorset landscape in the foreground.

of heathland that were the inspiration for Hardy's Egdon Heath were already under attack by the time he wrote the preface to the 1895 edition of *The Return of the Native*, in which he comments:

'Under the general name of "Egdon Heath," which has been given to the sombre scene of the story, are united or typified heaths of various real names, to the number of at least a dozen; these being virtually one in character and aspect, though their original unity, or partial unity, is now somewhat disguised by intrusive strips and slices brought under the plough with varying degrees of success, or planted to woodland.'

The process that was then in its early stages has now wiped out most of the heathland, but anyone who has been to lucky enough to visit any that remains

23

will immediately recognise the setting of *The Return of the Native* and understand Hardy's feelings about it.

'A Saturday afternoon in November was approaching the time of twilight, and the vast tract of unenclosed wild known as Egdon Heath embrowned itself moment by moment. Overhead the hollow stretch of whitish cloud shutting out the sky was as a tent which had the whole heath for its floor.

'The heaven being spread with this pallid screen and the earth with the darkest vegetation, their meeting-line at the horizon was clearly marked. In such contrast the heath wore the appearance of an instalment of night which had taken up its place before its astronomical hour was come: darkness had to a great extent arrived hereon, while day stood distinct in the sky. Looking upwards, a furze-cutter would have been inclined to continue work; looking down, he would have decided to finish his faggot and go home. The distant rims of the world and of the firmament seemed to be a division in time no less than a division in matter. The face of the heath by its mere complexion added half an hour to evening; it could in like manner retard the dawn, sadden noon, anticipate the frowning of storms scarcely generated, and intensify the opacity of a moonless midnight to a cause of shaking and dread.

'In fact, precisely at this transitional point of its nightly roll into darkness the great and particular glory of the Egdon waste began, and nobody could be said to understand the heath who had not been there at such a time. It could best be felt when it could not clearly be seen, its complete effect and explanation lying in this and the succeeding hours before the next dawn: then, and only then, did it tell its true tale. The spot was, indeed, a near relation of night, and when night showed itself an apparent tendency to gravitate together could be perceived in its shades and the scene. The sombre stretch of rounds and hollows seemed to rise and meet the evening gloom in pure sympathy, the heath exhaling darkness as rapidly as the heavens precipitated it. And so the obscurity in the air and the obscurity in the land closed together in a black fraternization towards which each advanced half-way.

'The place became full of a watchful intentness now; for when other things sank brooding to sleep the heath appeared slowly to awake and listen. Every night its Titanic form seemed to await something; but it had waited thus, unmoved, during so many centuries, through the crises of so many things, that it could only be imagined to await one last crisis—the final overthrow.

'It was a spot which returned upon the memory of those who loved it with an aspect of peculiar and kindly congruity. Smiling champaigns of flowers and fruit hardly do this, for they are permanently harmonious only with an existence of better reputation as to its issues than the present. Twilight combined with the scenery of Egdon Heath to evolve a thing majestic without severity, impressive without showiness, emphatic in its admonitions, grand in its simplicity. The qualifications which frequently invest the façade of a prison with far more dignity than is found in the façade of a palace double its size lent to this heath a sublimity in which spots renowned for beauty of the accepted kind are utterly wanting... Haggard Egdon appealed to a subtler and scarcer instinct, to a more recently learnt emotion, than that which responds to the sort of beauty called charming and fair...

'The most thorough-going ascetic could feel that he had a natural right to wander on Egdon: he was keeping within the line of legitimate indulgence when he laid himself open to influences such as these. Colours and beauties so far subdued were, at least, the birthright of all. Only in summer days of highest feather did its mood touch the level of gaiety. Intensity was more usually reached by way of the solemn than by way of the brilliant, and such a sort of intensity was often arrived at during winter darkness, tempests, and mists. Then Egdon was aroused to reciprocity; for the storm was its lover, and the wind its friend. Then it became the home of strange phantoms; and it was found to be the hitherto unrecognized original of those wild regions of obscurity which are vaguely felt to be compassing us about in midnight dreams of flight and disaster, and are never thought of after the dream till revived by scenes like this.

'It was at present a place perfectly accordant with man's nature—neither ghastly, hateful, nor ugly: neither commonplace, unmeaning, nor tame; but, like man, slighted and enduring; and withal singularly colossal and mysterious in its swarthy monotony. As with some persons who have long lived apart, solitude seemed to look out of its countenance. It had a lonely face, suggesting tragical possibilities...

'To recline on a stump of thorn in the central valley of Egdon, between afternoon and night, as now, where the eye could reach nothing of the world outside the summits and shoulders of heathland which filled the whole circumference of its glance, and to know that everything around and underneath had been from prehistoric times as unaltered as the stars overhead, gave ballast to the mind adrift on change, and harassed by the irrepressible New. The great inviolate place had an ancient permanence which the sea cannot claim. Who can say of a particular sea that it is old? Distilled by the sun, kneaded by the moon, it is renewed in a year, in a day, or in an hour. The sea changed, the fields changed, the rivers, the villages, and the people changed, yet Egdon remained. Those surfaces were neither so steep as to be destructible by weather, nor so flat as to be the victims of floods and deposits. With the exception of an aged highway, and a still more aged barrow...—themselves almost crystallized to natural products by long continuance—even the trifling irregularities were not caused by pickaxe, plough, or spade, but remained as the very finger-touches of the last geological change.'

25

The other aspect of Hardy that particularly appeals to me apart from his love of the countryside and its people is his concern with architecture, mainly ecclesiastical architecture. Although I did not know it until I started to read about Hardy's early life, this is something that I have in common with him, as well as with Stephen Smith, the hero of *A Pair of Blue Eyes*, who is sent to Endelstow (based largely on St Juliot in Cornwall) to make drawings of the parish church with a view to its restoration. Hardy's one job was to go around sketching and restoring the fabric of churches for an architect, while mine concerned all the other aspects of church restoration—designing and executing woodcarvings and church furnishings, and working on everything from sculpture and mosaic through engraved and stained glass to altar frontals, banners and vestments.

Like Hardy, too, I have been inspired by the later works of J.M.W. Turner, from that great period of experiment when Turner's contemporaries warned students not to go near him, as they believed him to be mad. I remember reading in a biography of Hardy's fascination with Turner and thinking that this was inevitable. If you become interested in a writer, an artist or a composer, it is likely that you will share with him an underlying attraction towards the same sort of work, the same tones or the same sounds.

In this book, I have aimed to explore my feelings for Dorset, using Hardy's portrait of it as a starting point. Over a period of two years or so, I have searched for images that echo the words of Hardy for me, looking at the landscape, the wildlife, the architecture and the people of the county. I have concentrated on an area of about twenty miles around Dorchester, a town that is a focus for me, as it was for Hardy. The area includes the Marshwood Vale in the west, Shaftesbury in the north, Wool in the east and the spectacular Dorset coastline in the south. In searching, I have sought to identify the spirit rather than the specific details of Hardy country, although I have shown some of the more famous Hardy locations where they have attracted me visually. The purpose of this book is not to track down and identify Hardy locations—Hermann Lea did that in 1913 with the help of Hardy himself and, in doing so, demonstrated the limits of such an enterprise by showing how much of the detail Hardy had moved around or changed while being true to the spirit of the place. My aim has been to capture the flavour of an area that still rings with the words of Hardy and is an endless source of inspiration to me as a painter. Having devoted myself to painting Hardy country so intensively, I am passionately concerned to make sure that it survives—too much irreparable damage has been done already. I therefore want to dedicate this book to the Dorset countryside and, above all, to its survival.

Gordon Beningfield
June 1983

I

THOMAS HARDY
AND HIS WORK

Thomas Hardy's early years were spent in a setting as rustic as any in his novels. Son of a master mason, he was born in 1840 in the Dorset village of Higher Bockhampton. As a boy, he learned ballads at his mother's knee and fiddle playing at his father's. He was a bright lad, a favourite of the great lady of the parish, educated in the village and in the county town, Dorchester. At sixteen, he was apprenticed to an architect and church restorer in the town, where he formed a friendship with the Dorset poet William Barnes, who was keeping a school in the adjoining house. When Hardy gained a place in a London firm of architects, he divided his leisure time between explorations of the city, friendships with his young colleagues, keeping up his music and his

Lower Bockhampton, in the Frome Valley below Hardy's birthplace. The first school he attended was in the building on the left of the picture, now a private house. I was there in the late afternoon of a still, crisp autumn day, when the smoke from the chimneys went straight up, and the rooks were flying across to the woodlands near Higher Bockhampton.

Hardy's birthplace at Higher Bockhampton. It was built by his grandfather on the edge of some of the heathland that appears in the novels as Egdon Heath. When I painted it, I tried to stand back and give an impression of it very much as it would have been in Hardy's day. There would have been a rather rambling garden with fruit trees and thickish hedgerows. Some of the beech trees that grew around it still survive, but now when you leave the back of the cottage, expecting to find heathland, you see nothing but Forestry Commission Christmas trees.

Greek and Latin, and writing letters to his favourite sister at home. There were loves, mainly undeclared, for village maidens and London beauties, and an engagement to a cousin.

When Hardy was thirty, he received a commission to work on the restoration of a church at St Juliot in North Cornwall, a region that he had always considered romantic—the Lyonesse of Arthurian legend. This was the assignment from which he returned 'with magic in his eyes', because he had encountered not just some interesting work and some fine scenery, but also Emma Gifford, who was to become the first Mrs Hardy.

Meanwhile, in London, his literary adventures had begun. Hardy's first novel, *The Poor Man and the Lady*, was rejected by Macmillan, but with strong encouragement to write another. At Chapman and Hall, the unknown young writer had the unusual luck of an interview with the publisher's reader, the novelist George Meredith, who offered him friendly professional advice. Meredith was of the opinion that a new author should not offend his potential readers with the views he expressed in his first book and that a novel was all the better for having plenty of plot. Taking these ideas to heart, Hardy tried

Stinsford Church, which is Mellstock Church in *Under the Greenwood Tree*, has strong links with Hardy and his family: his parents are buried there and his heart was placed there. His father played the fiddle for church services in a string choir like the one in the novel.

Right:
The room in the cottage at Higher Bockhampton where Hardy did much of his early writing.

31

Near Rampisham. A typical Dorset thatched cottage and a simple fence, the sort of sight that Hardy might have seen as he cycled around the countryside.

Left:
Two views of Max Gate, the house that Hardy had built near Dorchester, with the large bushes that he planted for privacy. Hardy designed the house himself and he kept adding to it, making a rear extension that became his study.

again, and 1871 saw the appearance of his first published work, *Desperate Remedies*, a novel that was on the whole not badly received. One reviewer, however, wrote that the book could only be 'a desperate remedy for an emaciated purse', a comment that made Hardy wish he were dead.

During this time, there was much correspondence with Emma Gifford, as well as some visits to Cornwall. *Under the Greenwood Tree*, published in 1872, was a complete success, as was *A Pair of Blue Eyes* in 1873. In 1874, when *Far from the Madding Crowd* was first appearing, Leslie Stephen, the editor of *The Cornhill Magazine*, in which the novel was serialised, wrote to Hardy:

'I am glad to congratulate you on the reception of your first number. Besides the gentle *Spectator*, which thinks that you must be George Eliot because you know the names of the stars, several good judges have spoken to me warmly of the *Madding Crowd*.'

There was no longer anything to stop the young man being entirely delighted to be alive, and Thomas and Emma were married with nothing worse to worry about than the division of their time between London and the country. Ahead were the fruits of success: the writing of the later novels, the amassing of a considerable fortune, the building of a substantial country house, Max Gate, near Dorchester, and easy friendships on equal terms with distinguished men and women in the literary world and outside it. With the years, however, also came a great deal of reflection, some disillusion and some grief.

Childless Emma in middle age was not the same wind-blown, pony-riding maiden who had copied his early manuscripts. She could often, in fact, be quite irritating, displaying a mind of her own; sometimes she was even ill. Hardy's liking for London social life in the season bordered on the gleeful, and occasionally Emma remained alone at Max Gate. Once she went to London alone and marched as a suffragette. But the bonds seem to have been as strong as the dissatisfactions—the couple were still going for bicycle rides with their friends over four counties in the last year of the nineteenth century.

At Max Gate, Hardy often brooded on the past and future of mankind, especially of Europe. And there were personal storm clouds gathering too. His best friend from his student days had killed himself. The cousin who had been his first fiancée—long a married woman—died, and Hardy grieved for her, their lost love and his lost youth. Emma disapproved of *Jude the Obscure*.

In 1912, Emma died, and he mourned her in poem after poem for the rest of his life, even imagining, or recreating, a reproachful voice, as in his poem *An Upbraiding*:

> Now I am dead you sing to me
>   The songs we used to know,
> But while I lived you had no wish
>   Or care for doing so
>
> Now I am dead you come to me
>   In the moonlight, comfortless;
> Ah, what would I have given alive
>   To win such tenderness!
>
> When you are dead, and stand to me
>   Not differenced as now,
> But like again, will you be cold
>   As when we lived, or how?

Near the base of Eggardon Hill, one of the many unmade tracks that wind across the landscape of Dorset.

Left:
A heron, painted as I might see one on a misty morning in the Frome Valley. It is the moment before he sees me and takes off, when I can only see the upper part of him.

Hardy's second wife, Florence Dugdale, was a loyal scribe and nurse, writing a biography of him to his close specification and caring for him as he grew old. She would, perhaps, have preferred to have remained the inspiration and source of joy that she had been to Hardy when he first knew her, before Emma's death. Neither the first nor the second Mrs Hardy found it easy to come to terms with living under the shadow of Hardy's fame as well as in its reflected glory, and the second Mrs Hardy also had to cope with the shadow of the first.

After the publication of his last novel, *Jude the Obscure*, in 1895 and the public fury it aroused, Hardy turned to writing poetry. It was easier, he maintained, to slip truth into poetry than into novels, even when the truth was autobiographical. He held that if Galileo had written in verse that the earth moved, no-one would have objected.

He worked immensely hard on the unpublished poems that he had been producing all his life, and on new ones, including his verse dramas, *The Dynasts* and *The Famous Tragedy of the Queen of Cornwall*. The poems were welcomed by the public as bright new stars in his crown. The world, including royalty, trooped to Max Gate to see him. Literary and academic honours were showered upon him. In 1910, he received the Order of Merit at Buckingham Palace on the same day as Sir Edward Elgar. He thought it all over and wrote a poem entitled *He Never Expected Much* as a reflection on his eighty-sixth birthday:

> Well, World, you have kept faith with me,
>   Kept faith with me;
> Upon the whole you have proved to be
>   Much as you said you were.
> Since as a child I used to lie
> Upon the leaze and watch the sky,
> Never, I own, expected I
>   That life would all be fair.
>
> 'Twas then you said, and since have said,
>   Times since have said,
> In that mysterious voice you shed
>   From clouds and hills around:...
>
> 'I do not promise overmuch,
>   Child; overmuch;
> Just neutral-tinted haps and such,'...

Florence Hardy said that her husband was never happier in his old age than when writing a gloomy poem. Equally, when he was younger, he had liked to include a poignant or tragic element in his novels, but the moods and happenings of his work are not simply the expression of an idyllic childhood followed by the disappointments of adult life.

Hardy was far more in control of his material than that. He was a Victorian novelist who had taken pains to learn his craft. He had accepted George Meredith's advice, and he had taken other advice too. He knew better than to write a novel made up of 'neutral-tinted haps'—such subject matter was a luxury that he saved for his poetry, after the work of fiction was done. For his novels, he used all the strong, arresting colours he could find, including black.

Working very hard at the craft of fiction, he faced up to the requirements of successful writing. As a young man, he wrote to Leslie Stephen:

The landscape of *The Woodlanders*. On High Stoy, near Minterne Magna, looking towards Dogbury Hill.

'The truth is that I am willing, and indeed anxious, to give up any points which may be desirable in a story when read as a whole, for the sake of others which shall please those who read it in numbers. Perhaps I may have higher aims some day, and be a great stickler for the proper artistic balance of the completed work, but for the present circumstances lead me to wish merely to be considered a good hand at a serial.'

When necessary, he would produce the plot that magazine serialisation demanded, writing towards successive peaks of interest to keep the reader's

attention engaged. From time to time, he went energetically through the editorial wrangles familiar to many Victorian authors over matters of sexual propriety. On the whole, everyone benefited—morality was upheld, publishers kept their readers, and the author was put on his mettle; if he were checked in one respect, he generally got his way in another.

Then, when Hardy found that his early work had put him fairly in the way of success, he had to face the next hurdle: he was, as Florence Hardy's biography tells us, 'committed by circumstances to novel-writing as a regular trade, as much as he had formerly been to architecture...' This was the real test. Much worse than paying attention to the special needs of serialisation (or of Mrs Grundy) would be boredom. It was boredom that would assail him if

My first sight of the farm near Corfe Castle which was exactly the sort of small, traditional Dorset farm I was hoping to find, with geese and chickens walking around and foraging in the farmyard.

he were prevented from writing what he wanted to write as his moods varied and his thought deepened, especially as he knew that he enjoyed writing tragedies as well as comedies. He knew that his readers wanted him to provide endless sunny tales of shepherd life; up to a point, he was going to thwart them.

He would give them enough of the countryside, which was his chosen setting for his thoughts. He would play the editors' game—handle seductions with delicacy, anguish the consciences of heroines about the minutiae of marital proprieties—but nothing, not even the wishes of his public, was going to prevent him from writing the scenes he wanted to write. He would give his readers an entrancing picture of the rustic and mostly innocent pleasures of

The rolling Dorset downland, ridged as a result of centuries of grazing by sheep. The view here is of one of the many butt-ended coombes, seen from the vantage point of Eggardon Hill.

pretty milkmaids in *Tess of the D'Urbervilles*; but he would also write of Tess wandering with Angel Clare cross country to windy Stonehenge, Tess's pursuers at their heels, the couple lapped in a sort of bliss because 'Tenderness was absolutely dominant in Clare at last.'

He would take his readers through the forests and orchards of *The Woodlanders*, to eavesdrop with him on the gossip and jokes of the workfolk; but he would also write Marty South's final speech at Giles Winterborne's grave:

'...whenever I get up I'll think of 'ee, and whenever I lie down I'll think of 'ee. Whenever I plant the young larches I'll think that none can plant as you planted; and whenever I split a gad, and whenever I turn the cider wring, I'll say none can do it like you. If ever I forget your name let me forget home and heaven!... But no, no, my love, I never can forget 'ee; for you was a good man, and did good things!'

He would write, too, of good men who sometimes did bad things, like Michael Henchard, the Mayor of Casterbridge, and of bad men who did bad things —Aeneas Manston in *Desperate Remedies*, Edred Fitzpiers in *The Woodlanders*, Damon Wildeve in *The Return of the Native*, and Alec D'Urberville. He would write of the ardours and ambitions of youth, but he would also lay before the reader Jude's ordeals, among which was the whole clumsy, savage, red-handed process of killing a pig.

Little by little, he won the right to say anything he wanted to say in prose (or in poetry when the change attracted him), because, from the time that *Under the Greenwood Tree* proved he had learned his trade, he had had his readers firmly in the hollow of his hand, in Wessex. When they got there —and they could not keep away—things might not always have been as they liked them, but this was no longer a main preoccupation of the man who had once been patronisingly called 'the good little Thomas Hardy' by Henry James. Hardy the great writer was no longer concerned simply to please his audience.

Early in life, he had decided what he liked and found his moral preferences as a writer. He preferred the light-hearted to the self-absorbed, the tolerant to the invidious, and above all he liked the spectacle of people throwing themselves wholeheartedly into whatever the Lord set before them—into any activity in which intelligence, physical effort and a clear understanding could be harnessed together towards a happy outcome, leaving proper room for the joys of the natural world and of human love.

In maturity, these things remained important to him, but as his sureness of his powers as a writer, his reliance on his readers and his experience of the world developed, he made some modifications in his attitude.

Very regretfully, for one who was so at home in his village church, he admitted disbelief in the whole idea of the Lord as Giver. The problem of pain

The churchyard of Stoke Abbott, a village on the edge of Marshwood Vale. I went to look at the church itself, but decided not to include it in the picture when I found the image of the sheep grazing among the tombstones, with the sun going down.

and suffering on earth was one to which he found no wholly satisfactory answer in Christian theology. Increasingly, he valued what he called 'the local cult of Christianity', chiefly for its unique message of 'loving-kindness'. Otherwise, he grew to feel that Christianity was outdated. He did not feel that he deserved any reproaches for his agnosticism; a truer accusation he felt, would be that he remained obstinately 'churchy' in his writings and leanings.

Light-heartedness, a welcoming attitude to life, never lost his approval, but on the subject of tolerance he became stretched in various directions. He did not forget that Mrs Grundy had been a nuisance; he felt that too much vigilance was exerted in protecting the technical virtue of women and too little in alleviating the pressures they were under—here he would have liked more tolerance and less hypocrisy.

He was finding it difficult himself to extend tolerance towards human behaviour—to look with loving-kindness at a world which rated that virtue so low. Having begun life with a Victorian faith in progress, he shared the awareness of the major Victorian novelists of the danger of material advances outstripping moral enlightenment. The outbreak of World War I, which he had not foreseen, confirmed his most serious doubts about the progress of humanity. Improvement was not taking place, but then, in spite of this major disappointment, nothing was actually any worse. In 1915, he wrote his poem *In Time of 'The Breaking of Nations'*:

West Stafford Church, the first sketch I did for this book. It is the church that Hardy had in mind as the place where Tess and Angel Clare were married.

A horse and cart with the old man who still uses them. He just stood there, apparently not taking much notice of what went on around him.

I

Only a man harrowing clods
        In a slow silent walk
With an old horse that stumbles and nods
        Half asleep as they stalk

II

Only thin smoke without flame
        From the heaps of couch-grass:
Yet this will go onward the same
        Though Dynasties pass.

III

Yonder a maid and her wight
        Come whispering by:
War's annals will cloud into night
        Ere their story die.

Pity and intelligence, nature and human nature could be counted on; Hardy had long accepted that a happy ending could not.

The Mayor of Casterbridge gets little for his efforts to prosper and to do people justice. Clym Yeobright in *The Return of the Native* fails, like everyone else, to teach the poor and ignorant to face their destinies better. Often, 'the critical question is not answered at the critical time.' When the young Jude lies disconsolately longing for someone to come to help with his perplexities, 'nobody did come, because nobody does...' Love, that device of all devices provided for the solace of humanity, may be wasted or betrayed. As Grace turns back to Edred in *The Woodlanders* for the sake of the sacrament of marriage, Giles, the deserving, is unrewarded. The finely poised may go as wrong as the coarse-grained; in *Jude the Obscure*, Sue Bridehead's way of loving hurts as much as Arabella's.

Hardy had tempted his readers into Wessex with a vision of village fiddlers, blushing maidens, shepherd's crooks and painted wagons piled high with harvests of wheat and shining cider apples. But by the end of the novels, he had revealed that it contained deceit and squalor as well as work and hope and happiness. Egdon was King Lear's blasted heath as well as the grassy home of bees and butterflies.

It was all quite deliberate. Hardy wanted to show the difference between the good and bad things of life, and he did not care to do it by leaving out the bad.

Dorset heathland.

II

HARDY'S WESSEX

Among the pieces of advice that Thomas Hardy took to heart as an aspiring novelist was a remark made by the historian and writer John Morley about *The Poor Man and the Lady*, that 'the country scenes were the best in the book', and he set the whole of his next novel in a Dorset village.

Its setting in time was Hardy's childhood and took in his earliest memories, including his father's and his grandfather's reminiscences as well as his own experience, especially of the musical life of the village. Every detail of the music, of the instruments used by the players, every cottage and every hedgerow came from this background. Hardy wanted to call the novel *Mellstock Quire, A Rural Painting of the Dutch School*, but the publisher's idea of a reference to *As You Like It* was adopted, and the book appeared as *Under the Greenwood Tree*.

Hardy's heroine, Fancy, is a girl as 'skittish' as the later Bathsheba of *Far from the Madding Crowd*, a young man's young woman, whose very ordinariness is full of mystery. Around her, Hardy shapes a village life full of work and

A cottage in south west Dorset, tucked into the bank of the coombe, with rough meadow land all around it. One of Hardy's farm workers might well have lived in this sort of cottage.

November near Cattistock. It was the weather that attracted me here—Hardy was so good at using words to catch the mood of the weather and the landscape. I was walking down the track, looking for a suitable subject, when there was a sudden change of weather. It had been quite bright, then a wind picked up, a dark cloud came over, and the last remaining leaves were being blown from the trees and the hedgerows. This was the moment between the sunlight and the dark, overhanging cloud.

music, with time for celebrations, good drink, old carols, dancing, for proper attention to old and young, for listening to the wise and rebuking the foolish. It is a book full of kindness—the feeble Thomas Leaf, perpetually hovering on the outskirts of activities in a tremble of regret at the happenings he is sure to be excluded from, exists only so that he can always be admitted at the last minute with the rest of the villagers. The community is comic but right-minded and full of common sense—it is seen as if through the eyes of a well-looked-after child, who is not too innocent to sense little ripples of adult snobberies, envies or regrets but who notices them only so that he can fit them into his enlarging view of human beings.

As the young Hardy repossessed his childhood and developed apparently without effort into a competent novelist, he took possession also of his countryside. The country that has become known as Hardy's Wessex is not purely fictional in the way that Anthony Trollope's Barsetshire is. When Trollope wrote of the 'new shire which I had added to the English counties,' and said of his sites that he knew all their accessories 'as though I had lived and wandered there,' he was speaking of a region with no other origin than his own imagination. Hardy's Wessex, on the other hand, is very close indeed to the real landscape of Dorset and its surrounding counties, although he manipulated it in ways that are tantalising for any reader inclined to be geographically precise. A village or a house or a tree may be identifiable, as may a cottage or an inn or a road, but it may also turn out in Hardy's writing to have moved closer to an adjoining town or river than the map would show.

Lulworth Cove, a natural harbour which is one of the finest sights of Dorset's spectacular coastline. In *Far from the Madding Crowd*, it is called Lulstead Cove and Troy goes for a swim there on the day after his visit to Fanny Robin's grave, and gets carried out to sea by the current.

An old path with a tiny gate that leads from one meadow into the next.

A stretch of landscape may be dotted or surrounded with towns or villages, some of which will appear under their own and some under fictional names.

Hardy claimed that his landscape was the entire ancient kingdom of Wessex—a territory that was historically of shifting shape—and he gave us guidelines for its borders. In the *General Preface to the Novels and Poems* for the Wessex edition of 1912, he described the 'province bounded on the north by the Thames, on the south by the English Channel, on the east by a line running from Hayling Island to Windsor Forest, and on the west by the Cornish coast...' The fictional Castle Boterel in Cornwall, however, lies near, or no great way beyond the border of the Wessex kingdom. Gloucester is just outside it. Oxford, Hardy's Christminster, has one toe almost within it.

Hardy's use of existing geography gives him enormous advantages as a writer. In the first place, his fictional map of Wessex floats above the real map with an authority of its own. Hardy's Wessex is not quite anybody else's

Wessex. Bath remains Bath—but then perhaps Hardy does not care very much about Bath in his novels, any more than he cares very much about London. Dorchester becomes Casterbridge, but whether this is because Dorchester never had a mayor called Michael Henchard and Hardy is not going to pretend that it did, we do not know. Egdon Heath is a fictional name used to describe several tracts of heathland that Hardy loved. But are the fictional names meant to disguise or give away identities—Emminster for Beaminster, Kingsbere for Bere Regis?

In his fiction, Hardy travelled at will within his own vision of the south-western counties, a vision composed of Wessex together with Lyonesse, a region to the west, somewhere beyond it or separate from it. Its features moved around at his convenience in much the way that the shapes of places

This sketch shows the traditional texture of the countryside in south west Dorset with the hedge-rows and thickets that could so easily have been grubbed out, but still survive and are full of wildlife.

Evershot, Hardy's Evershead, with the cottage that is now known as Tess's Cottage because it can be identified as the one where the heroine of *Tess of the D'Urbervilles* stopped and took breakfast on her walk to Angel Clare's home. I like the combination of the simple Dorset cob and thatch of the cottage with the ecclesiastical sharpness of the Gothic church butting up against it.

and landscapes shift in people's individual memories. Within this framework, he was free to record the details of nature with absolute accuracy, as well as the details of dialect, seasons, customs, country tasks, and the social arrangements of the countryside. Hardy's Wessex gave him what every novelist has to find in one way or another: a space where he can both record meticulously and invent freely.

51

To have a region of his own was a considerable asset to a novelist who was not a Londoner and who was not fascinated by London. He could not hold up a mirror to the London-centred public that read novels, but the public was prepared to overlook this in an author who would tell them instead about something they did not know, or only thought they knew, or knew only a little. Hardy took them far deeper into country life than they had ever dreamed of going.

This impressive package of a semi-fictional countryside that would appeal to his readers but could be easily manipulated by the author was arrived at cautiously by the young Hardy, and for a young man's reasons. Florence

Looking away from Tess's Cottage, past Evershot Church and down through the village. It is a place where you can still stand in the middle of the road without being killed.

The village of Puddletown, Hardy's Weatherbury in *Far from the Madding Crowd*.

Hardy mentions 'Hardy's wilful purpose in his early novels until *Far from the Madding Crowd* appeared, if not later, having been to mystify the reader as to their locality, origin and authorship by various interchanges and inventions…' As a conscientious recorder, she goes on to explain that this was not due to creative caprice but '…probably owing at first to his doubt if he would pursue the craft, and his sense of the shadow that would fall on an architect who had failed as a novelist.' It was not only artistry that was guiding him, but common sense. The young man meant to succeed, if not as a writer, then in architecture, for which he had been trained. In the novels, we often see a man taking up a new way of life with cheerful resolution when his initial ambition has failed him. As it happened, Hardy did not fail at the profession of novelist, and the countryside he adopted became the customary background for his fiction. In *Far from the Madding Crowd*, he marked this countryside for the first time with the name of Wessex, and for *The Return of the Native*, he drew his own map of it.

In *Far from the Madding Crowd*, Gabriel Oak had his hut on Norcombe Hill. This is identified as being on Toller Down, so I went there and searched for a shepherd's hut. I saw an old man walking across a field and asked him if he knew of any shepherds' huts. Pointing to a wood in the distance, he told me that there had been a hut there 27 years ago. He suggested I should ask at the estate office, but when I did, I found that the hut had been sold three years before to a retired builder who lives in Cattistock. When I got there, I discovered a workshop from which a tapping sound was emerging. I walked in to find an old man in a three-piece suit, complete with watch chain, planing a piece of wood. After I had explained why I was there, the man took me round the corner of the workshop, and there stood the shepherd's hut. The reason he had wanted it was that as a little boy he had sat in it with the shepherds on Toller Down. Now this old man, who is well into his seventies, has an armchair in it and sits there in the evenings, much to the annoyance of his wife.

For most readers, it is enough, as it always was, to wander in Hardy's countryside, noting here and there an identifiable landmark as an extra point of interest. One admirer of the novels, though, would be satisfied only by the most precise information that he could possibly discover about the lie of Hardy's land. In the novelist's later years, the young Hermann Lea sought his acquaintance. He made excursions through Wessex with Hardy to pursue his investigations and get his questions answered. With Hardy's permission and help, he produced his book *Hardy's Wessex* and the most inquiring detective is unlikely to garner more information than he sets out. It was detail that Lea was after: Hardy's Evershead in *Tess of the D'Urbervilles* is based on the village of Evershot, and you can still see the church; in *Far from the Madding Crowd*, Puddletown, with its church, is the model, slightly displaced, for Weatherbury, and Norcombe Hill, the site of Gabriel Oak's shepherd's hut, can be identified as being on Toller Down, to the west of Rampisham. Grace's wedding dress in *The Woodlanders* comes from Exonbury, which is in very nearly the same place as Exeter. The hill fortress of Eggar in the poem *My Cicely* is the ancient earth castle of Eggardon. Hardy's birthplace, Higher Bockhampton, is combined with Lower Bockhampton and the whole parish of Stinsford to make the fictional Mellstock in *Under the Greenwood Tree* and other novels and poems. Mr Lea is a very useful companion in ranging over the Wessex of the novels. Mellstock is its spiritual centre, but the region is large and full of variety. Within Wessex, Hardy finds settings for his fiction with as many differing and clearly defined atmospheres as any novelist could need, and he varies the locale from book to book.

His preference was to be in Wessex when he was writing a Wessex novel, but this does not mean that he painted only what he could see from his window. Early in his married life with Emma, he was living in a rented house

Heathland is a very important part of Hardy's landscape, but today it is quite hard to find in Dorset, as most of it has been ploughed up or planted with Christmas trees. This piece of heathland is near the atomic station at Winfrith.

in Sturminster Newton in the north of Dorset—an idyll, Emma called it, and 'our happiest time'. His second wife records '...the rich alluvial district of Sturminster Newton in which the author was now living was not used by him at this time as a setting for the story he was constructing there, but the heath country twenty miles off.' The novel was *The Return of the Native* and the country Egdon Heath, the composite name for the moorland between Dorchester and Bournemouth or, in Hardy's terms, between Casterbridge and Sandbourne. Living at Wimborne, he wrote *Two on a Tower*, which was set locally. *The Mayor of Casterbridge* was written while Hardy was supervising the building of his new house, Max Gate, a mile outside Dorchester. In this house he wrote *The Woodlanders*, set, as Lea points out, in '...the

Marnhull, which Hardy called Marlott, is the small village near Shaftesbury where the beginning of *Tess of the D'Urbervilles* is set. I tried to think where Hardy would have imagined or seen the May Day dance taking place, with the village girls in their white dresses, and I think it might have been here.

A cottage with a great explosion of roses filling its front garden. It reminded me of the days when gardeners were perhaps not as clinical as they are today.

You can still find properly laid hedges in Dorset, where they are not just hacked back with flails. This sketch, which suggests the great skill that goes into laying hedges, was made in April. The laying would have been done not too long before, at the end of the winter.

northern portion of the county of Dorset—or South Wessex as it is termed in these books—on the outskirts of the Blackmoor Vale.' *Tess of the D'Urbervilles*, which ranges from 'Salisbury Plain in the north to Dorchester in the south; from the New Forest in the east to Beaminster in the west,' was also written at Max Gate, as was *Jude the Obscure*, which was set 'in the northern portion of Wessex', between Oxford and Great Fawley (Christminster and Marygreen), branching out to Melchester, Shaston and Aldbrickham (Salisbury, Shaftesbury and Reading). At Max Gate, too, Hardy wrote his poetry, including *The Dynasts*, which roves over Napoleon's Europe as well as parts of Wessex, and *The Famous Tragedy of the Queen of Cornwall*, set once more in Lyonesse.

Following Lea, who gained Hardy's not quite wholehearted concurrence in the project, we can identify roads, walks, villages, cottages, inns, towns and great houses, sometimes not much changed, as the origin of many of Hardy's details. Hardy's picture of Wessex, which was in his head and is in the novels, cannot be pinned down like a replica on a sheet of tracing paper over a geographer's map of south-western England, and Lea is the first to admit it.

Right:
Cottage windows in the Marshwood Vale. As I walked through the village, I was attracted by the geraniums and other flowers in the windows. My grandmother always had plants like that, and there is a reference at the beginning of *Far from the Madding Crowd* to the load on Bathsheba's wagon including 'window plants', among them 'myrtles, geraniums and cactuses'.

Overleaf:
Dorset Horn sheep.

58

III
THE PAST PRESERVED

When Hardy looked at his countryside, its history was no less present than its geography in his mind. The landmarks from the past, which his characters for the most part found so familiar that they took them for granted as part of the daily scene, were pondered on by Hardy for what they had been in their time. He points out that Elizabeth-Jane in *The Mayor of Casterbridge* takes her walks a quarter of a mile away from the prehistoric fort of Mai Dun. He finds it satisfactory that the villagers in *The Return of the Native* make their bonfires on that part of Egdon Heath called Rainbarrow, a site so ancient that, seeing a figure on it, 'The first instinct of an imaginative stranger might have been to suppose it the person of one of the Celts who built the barrow...' Before the shadowy fire-lit figures are allowed to reveal themselves as gossiping nineteenth-century villagers, the imaginative stranger persists in his thinking:

I found this view of the Blackmoor Vale when I was travelling up from Evershot to see the Cross-in-Hand, and turned to look across this great vista dotted with small farms. The one change in the view since Hardy's day is the planting of Christmas trees, but as they were there, I felt that I should include them in the picture.

'It was as if these men and boys had suddenly dived into past ages and fetched therefrom an hour and deed which had before been familiar with this spot. The ashes of the original British pyre which blazed from that summit lay fresh and undisturbed in the barrow beneath their tread. The flames from funeral piles long ago kindled there had shone down upon the lowlands as these were shining now. Festival fires to Thor and Woden had followed on the same ground and duly had their day… Moreover to light a fire is the instinctive and resistant act of man when, at the winter ingress, the curfew is sounded throughout Nature… Black chaos comes, and the fettered gods of the earth say, Let there be light.'

The imaginative stranger, Hardy, has pulled the reader back through many centuries and generations before the villagers, who are neither especially

Corfe Castle on the Isle of Purbeck, called Corvesgate Castle by Hardy.

imaginative nor indeed educated to perceive a past beyond Christendom, begin singing their songs and discussing the day's business of a village wedding. Their sense of the past is random and hardly articulated. In *Far from the Madding Crowd*, Hardy writes, 'In these Wessex nooks the busy outsider's ancient times are only old; his old times are still new; his present is futurity.' The building of Hardy's house at Max Gate threw up Roman relics, which were fresh in his mind as he was writing *The Mayor of Casterbridge*:

'The Ring at Casterbridge was merely the local name of one of the finest Roman Amphitheaters, if not the very finest, remaining in Britain.

'Casterbridge announced old Rome in every street, alley, and precinct. It looked Roman, bespoke the art of Rome, concealed dead men of Rome. It was impossible to dig more than a foot or two deep about the town fields and gardens without coming upon some tall soldier or other of the Empire, who had lain there in his silent unobtrusive rest for a space of fifteeen hundred years.'

To Hardy, what was past was never completely lost:

'...some old people said that at certain moments in the summer time, in broad daylight, persons sitting with a book or dozing in the arena had, on lifting their eyes, beheld the slopes lined with a gazing legion of Hadrian's soldiery as if watching the gladiatorial combat; and had heard the roar of their excited voices; that the scene would remain but a moment, like a lightning flash, and then disappear.'

For the most part, the past which forms the background of Hardy's characters' present lives is the past of English Christendom: the ruined abbey with its still working mill in *Tess of the D'Urbervilles;* Weatherbury Farm in *Far from the Madding Crowd,* drawn to some extent from Waterston Manor:

'a hoary building, of the Jacobean stage of Classic Renaissance as regards its architecture, and of a proportion which told at a glance that, as is so frequently the case, it had once been the manorial hall upon a small estate around it...'

In the same book, the great shearing barn 'on ground-plan resembled a church with transepts, whose origins have been forgotten. It not only emulated the form of the neighbouring church of the parish, but vied with it in antiquity. Whether the barn had ever formed one of a group of conventual buildings nobody seemed to be aware; no trace of such surroundings remained. The vast porches at the sides, lofty enough to admit a waggon laden to its highest with corn in the sheaf, were spanned by heavy-pointed arches of stone, broadly and boldly cut...'

Waterston Manor, near Puddletown, was the model for Bathsheba's Weatherbury Farm in *Far from the Madding Crowd*. As it is hidden from the road by trees, I went down the lane and looked back across the fields to find this pleasing composition with part of the house visible and cows in the meadow.

Left:
The Cross-in-Hand, a small stone pillar on the road between Evershot and Minterne Magna, which appears in *Tess of the D'Urbervilles* as the stone on which Alec makes Tess put her hand when she swears never to tempt him.

The front of Miss Charmond's Hintock House in *The Woodlanders* is '...an ordinary manorial presentation of Elizabethan windows, mullioned and hooded, worked in rich snuff-coloured freestone...' and lies so securely in its hollow that a few sheep '...as they ruminated looked quietly into the bedroom windows'.

The humbler home of Dick Dewey and his father, the 'tranter', in *Under the Greenwood Tree*, '...a long low cottage with a hipped roof of thatch, having dormer windows breaking up into the eaves...' is already old, '...for the most part covered with creepers, though these were rather beaten back from the doorway—a feature which was worn and scratched by much passing in and

65

out, giving it by day the appearance of an old keyhole.' Hardy loved human habitations as much for themselves as for their significance in his novels; he once wrote '...clouds, mists and mountains are unimportant besides the wear on a threshold...'

Hardy loved churches, too, and was very much at home with them. Church architecture and its restoration had been the specialised part of his training, and had inspired him with a good deal of affection for architectural detail. He would use these details in his novels for a novelist's purposes, but he valued them both for their own sake and for the sense they gave him of being in touch across the generations with other men who had understood the same skills. In

The Abbey Barn at Abbotsbury, just inland from the west end of Chesil Beach, built by the monks who farmed the area so successfully. It is one of the barns in south Dorset that could have inspired the great barn that is used for sheep shearing in *Far from the Madding Crowd*. It would have been a perfect setting for a nineteenth-century harvest home.

Far from the Madding Crowd, the reader is being led to the graveyard where Fanny Robin is buried, and where the dashing Troy is to fail to decorate her grave with flowers as completely as he has failed to look after her in life. The reader is taken to the scene by way of some very accurate description of the work of the masters who had in their time created it. The details were assembled by Hardy with at least two churches in mind:

'The tower of Weatherbury Church was a square erection of fourteenth century date, having two stone gurgoyles on each of the four faces of its parapet... Weatherbury tower was a somewhat early instance of the use of an ornamental parapet in parish as distinct from cathedral churches, and the

A cottage near Powerstock set among trees and old meadow land.

Puddletown Church—Weatherbury Church,
where Fanny Robin is buried, in *Far from the
Madding Crowd*. This is my favourite view of it,
with the lamp over the gateway silhouetted against
the yew tree. For this reason, I have added some
body colour to make the lamp stand out.

gurgoyles which are the necessary correlatives of a parapet, were excep-
tionally prominent—of the boldest cut that the hand could shape, and of the
most original design that a human brain could conceive... This horrible stone
entity was fashioned as if covered with a wrinkled hide; it had short, erect
ears, eyes starting from their sockets, and its fingers and hands were seizing
the corners of its mouth, which they thus seemed to pull open to give passage
to the water it vomited...

    'Troy slept on in the porch, and the rain increased outside.'

The entrance porch to Puddletown Church. After working on the painting of the church from beside the rectory, I went into the churchyard and stood under the yew tree to sketch the porch. It was not here but in the other porch that Troy slept in *Far from the Madding Crowd*.

When he wakes to see that the 'gurgoyles' have flooded his flower arrangement and destroyed it, he vanishes from the villages, leaving Bathsheba to tend the grave and look after the repairs to the plumbing. Troy's business is with the passing moment, which is easy to mar but not to mend; Bathsheba's is to deal with the present bearing the future in mind; the novelist's is to link past, present and future together.

Apart from observing them with a novelist's eye, Hardy had a personal affection for the elements in country life, the customs and rituals, that formed

69

July in the Marshwood Vale, my first view of the harvest on this small, traditional farm. I had a telephone call to tell me that the corn was stooked and I rushed down to Dorset at 5 o'clock the next morning. When I arrived, I found myself looking at a landscape that reminded me of how the countryside around my home in Hertfordshire looked perhaps 35 years ago. There were big, full hedges with low, twisted old oak trees and rooks feeding on the stubble. It is an image of the countryside exactly as Hardy would have seen it. I sat down against one of the stooks with my sandwiches and spent the whole day doing the preliminary work for this picture.

Left:
A steam engine driving a thrashing machine at a show near Shaftesbury.

living links between past, of whatever period, and present. He knew that in his time he was observing a period of rapid change in rural life. The countryside observances of his childhood were things that he had always taken for granted, but he knew when he recorded them that he might be among the last in a position to do so.

The circle of the working year, which could include poverty, anxiety and disappointment, was studded with celebrations, which had a significance beyond helping to make life worth living. Each of these celebrations was undertaken with all the skill that the participants could muster. In spite of their carefree and often hard-drinking aspects, most of these festivals were religious in origin, some Christian and others pagan.

Under the Greenwood Tree opens on Christmas Eve with the tranter and his companions setting out to sing carols—including the old and beautiful

71

'Remember Adam's Fall'. The carol singing is protracted and takes its toll of the music the same fiddlers produce in church on Christmas Day. In *The Return of the Native*, a splendid party takes place on Christmas night, with lavish amounts of mead and elder wine, beef and bread, cake and pastry, and the mummers' performance. The villagers perform their carefully rehearsed play of Saint George:

More images of harvesting on the farm in the Marshwood Vale: the sheaves of corn being loaded on the trailer and the building of the rick with a grain elevator. I decided to conceal the tractor that drives the elevator. The farm dog followed me around the harvest field, chasing mice and popping out from behind the sheaves.

> 'Here come I, Saint George, the valiant man,
>   With naked sword and spear in hand,
> Who fought the dragon and brought him to the slaughter
> And by this won fair Sabra, the King of Egypt's daughter;
>   What mortal man would dare to stand
>   Before me with my sword in hand?'

A traditional thatched straw stack on a farm near Shipton Gorge, a few miles from Bridport. The rooks which had been scratching around for insects all burst out from behind the stack and scattered as I walked into the field.

Hardy points out that:

'A traditional pastime is to be distinguished from a mere revival in no more striking feature than in this, that while in the revival all is excitement and fervour, the survival is carried on with a stolidity and absence of stir which sets one wondering why a thing that is done so perfunctorily should be kept up at all...'

Right:
Meadow Sweet, a flower that I have always thought of as being particularly Victorian. It is found everywhere on soggy watermeadows.

The performance, like other events, was simply something that happened each year: 'Nobody commented, any more than they would have commented on the fact of mushrooms coming in autumn or snowdrops in spring.'

During the cold spring, from Candlemas to Lady Day, the agricultural work of the next season was organised. Lent and Easter were celebrated according to the rites of the Church, and May Day, another pagan rite, marked the beginning of the summer: '...the birch trees which grew on this margin of the vast Egdon wilderness had put on their new leaves, delicate as butterflies' wings, and diaphanous as amber,' wrote Hardy in *The Return of the Native*:

'Beside Fairway's dwelling was an open space recessed from the road, and here were now collected all the young people within a radius of a couple of miles. The pole lay with one end supported on a trestle, and women were engaged in wreathing it from the top downwards with wild-flowers... in these spots homage to nature, self-adoration, frantic gaieties, fragments of Teutonic rites to divinities whose names are forgotten, seem in some way or other to have survived mediaeval doctrine.'

Decorating the pole was a delicate and intricate matter:

'At the top of the pole were crossed hoops decked with small flowers; beneath these came a milk-white zone of Maybloom; then a zone of bluebells, then of cowslips, then of lilacs, then of ragged-robins, daffodils and so on...'

The dancing that takes place on the green is accompanied by an 'enthusiastic brass band'.

After May Day, it is not long until the sheep-shearing supper, to celebrate the conclusion of a sizeable and important piece of work. In *Far from the Madding Crowd*, on the first day of June, the workfolk look forward to 'some lordly junketing tonight' after observing 'great puddens in the milking pails... a great black crock upon the brandise...' and 'two bushels of biffins for apple pies... For the shearing-supper a long table was placed on the grass plot beside the house...'

During the summer, there are village picnics, 'gipsyings', as Eustacia Vye describes them in *The Return of the Native*, celebrations seemingly quite apart from the rhythms either of the Church year or of the working year. Late in August, in the open country outside the village, the East Egdon band plays in a flower-decked painted wagon and elderly dames prepare refreshments:

'A whole village-full of sensuous emotions, scattered abroad all year long, surged here in focus for an hour. The forty hearts of those waving couples were beating as they had not done since, twelve months before, they had come together in similar jollity. For the time Paganism was revived in their hearts, the pride of life was all in all, and they adored none other than themselves.'

A barn that could easily have been used for a harvest home. It is not far from Dorchester, on the Wareham road.

The working year brings another celebration at the end of August. At Bathsheba's farm in *Far from the Madding Crowd* comes the harvest supper, celebrated in the barn—one end piled high with oats and screened off with sailcloth—with fiddlers and a tambourine man on a rostrum, decorations of green foliage, cider and ale, and dancing.

With harvest home, the business of summer is accomplished. In the Autumn, cider is made, and nuts collected, evenings grow shorter, the bonfires blaze up against the dark and burn themselves out, the mummers are rehearsing again, and the year has come full circle.

This cycle of the labour, leisure and ritual of farm and village, touching wider worlds at the great fairs that linked the countryside, at weekly market-days in the little towns and at church, was a way of life worth recording, not

76

for its monotony, but for its liveliness and inventiveness and energy. Hardy, however, would not have wished to pass on a picture of Wessex life that was of unrelieved sweetness. Perhaps it was only in *Under the Greenwood Tree* that he wanted to sound that note.

Clym Yeobright, in *The Return of the Native*, is a good man. He loves his fellow mortals, and he loves the changing seasons on Egdon Heath as deeply as Eustacia loathes them. Yet, when he returns to his own people from his foreign travels, he is shocked by the lives he sees around him in the countryside. He wants to teach, to be 'a schoolmaster to the poor and ignorant, to teach them what nobody else will. He sees 'half the world going to ruin for want of somebody to buckle to and teach them how to breast the misery they are born to.'

Sheep fairs, like the one in *Far from the Madding Crowd*, often had fairgrounds to go with them. This is a traditional fun fair, which is also a traction engine show, that takes place every year near Shaftesbury. I have been to it a number of times, and it has always rained, which is why I have shown it with dark clouds building up and mud everywhere.

Another farm where the corn is harvested with binders, but here the ricks are covered with tarpaulins and the corn is shortly to be thrashed.

Left:
A typical Dorset cottage in a village near the Marshwood Vale, with a thatched porch and a wicker chair in the front garden.

Hardly has he finished outlining his plans to his mother than a neighbour appears with the interesting news that on that very morning '…Susan Nunsuch had pricked Miss Vye with a long stocking-needle, as she had threatened to do as soon as ever she could get the young lady to church, where she don't come very often… so as to draw her blood and put an end to the bewitching of Susan's children that has been carried on so long.'

Towards the end of the novel, and towards the end of Eustacia Vye's life, Susan '…busied herself with a ghastly invention of superstition, calculated to bring powerlessness, atrophy, and annihilation on any human being against whom it was directed. It was a practice well known in Egdon at that date, and one that is not quite extinct at the present day.' The details Hardy proceeds to give here of the making of a wax model are very precise. So, too, are those for its proper use: ' "Did you notice, my dear, [asks Susan gently of her sick child] what Mrs Eustacia wore this afternoon besides the dark dress?' "

The child has noticed, and a red ribbon and inked-in sandals are added to the model before Susan takes her pin-packet, thrusts as many as fifty pins into the image and holds it with tongs to melt over the heat of the fire, while she

This was the first time that I saw stooks in a field in Dorset. It was somewhere in the Frome Valley and started me on the search for the harvest scenes that I found for this book.

repeats the Lord's Prayer backwards three times, 'the incantation usual in proceedings for obtaining unhallowed assistance against an enemy.'

Clym would have liked to rid the country people of such beliefs and practices; Hardy makes it clear that the Wessex he portrays is not just the home of flowery maypoles and jovial harvest-homes, but also a countryside where witchcraft is practised, as well as other rites of variously sinister and superstitious import. Hangmen in the towns can earn extra gratuities by allowing sufferers from intractable diseases to touch the newly cut-down corpse (a practice known, reasonably, as turning the blood)—if no hanged man is available, a bag of toads at Toad Fair may do the same trick. Jude's wife can buy a love philtre and use it if not on one man, then on another. The good little Thomasin in *The Return of the Native*, whose marriage has been only slightly improperly delayed, is terrified, at the sound of approaching voices, that she and her betrothed are to be the objects of a 'skimmity ride'. At

Ordinary but still unspoilt Dorset countryside: a muddy track and fields with big hedgerows. I like the sort of improvisation that can be seen here with the piece of rustic timber and a strand of barbed wire.

Casterbridge, a life is lost because of a skimmington-ride, a savage romp where the effigies of a couple who have offended rural proprieties are displayed and pilloried. Furtive little journeys are made through woods by quite respectable people to conjurors, wise women and weather-prophets. A wife can be bought and sold and believe the transaction binding. An approaching letter can be seen in a candle's flame, and maidens can identify their future husbands on Midsummer Eve. At village churches, young men ring wedding bells for the funerals of unmarried girls so that death will not cheat them of their dues.

These practices reach back into the past as surely as the Roman ruins or the blazing bonfires. For Hardy, they were just as much a part of the present. He wrote in his *General Preface to the Novels and Poems* for the Wessex edition of 1912 that 'At the dates represented in the various narrations things were like that in Wessex: the inhabitants lived in certain ways, engaged in certain occupations, kept alive certain customs, just as they are shown doing in these pages.'

Puddletown Church: alabaster effigies which have connections with Hardy's poem *The Children and Sir Nameless*.

IV

THE PEOPLE OF
THE COUNTRYSIDE

Hardy's chosen material was the life of Wessex, which he knew so well, and he soon discovered that his audience was eager to be told more about it. Hardy engaged his readers' attention so skilfully that he was able to explain to them step by step that their preconceptions about country life had been ill-founded, and to offer them an entirely new set of facts and attitudes.

Hardy had a complicated relationship with his background. Although his origins were relatively humble, he was always ambitious in a way that would, if he were successful, lift him out of village life and into the companionship of educated people. In this new circle, Hardy succumbed increasingly to the temptation to highlight the aspects of his origin that would seem socially acceptable and to play down those that might be found lowly or mundane. He liked to give the impression that he had sprung from a family that was on the decline from past prosperity rather than from parents who had, in village terms, done unexpectedly well. There was a touch of harmless disloyalty to the facts in his presentation of his own beginnings.

Yellowham Wood makes various appearances in Hardy under the name of Yalbury Wood. The keeper's cottage was the home of Fancy and her family in *Under the Greenwood Tree*. When I visited it, there were pheasant coops in the garden.

84

However, when he spun the stuff of country life into his pastoral web of literary success, he was both loyal to the facts and accurate in his rendering of them. In his fiction, he conveyed his firmest sense of the realities of country life while instructing the townsfolk on their misapprehensions.

The town was mistaken, in the first place, about the nature of country people. Just as a yokel would be misguided to believe that the streets of London were paved with gold, so the townsperson was no less in error in thinking that Wessex labourers were all of one clay, hardly to be distinguished from one another. In his essay, *The Dorsetshire Labourer*, he spells out the point in non-fictional terms. He observes that the labouring class is '...a number of dissimilar fellow-creatures, men of many minds, infinite in difference; some happy, many serene, a few depressed; some clever, even to

In Cranborne Chase—The Chase in *Tess of the D'Urbervilles*. A hurdle-maker at work with his jacket hung up on a hazel branch. The whole wood, carpeted with bluebells and ringing with the sound of nightingales, gave him the feeling of working, he said, in heaven, and the wood is known as Heaven's Wood.

85

genius, some stupid, some wanton, some austere; some mutely Miltonic, some Cromwellian; …men who have private views of each other; …who applaud or condemn each other; amuse or sadden themselves by the contemplation of each other's foibles or vices…' Hardy insists that once they have been truly seen in this light by the townsman, 'they cannot be rolled together again…' He can refer in non-fiction to 'Dick the carter, Bob the shepherd and Sam the ploughman' as unique and distinguishable individuals, and the reader will take the point without any difficulty or indeed without any strong feelings. But in the novels, the reader understands wholeheartedly, not just without resistance, but without being conscious of the point being made at all.

The value and significance of the individual and of his chosen behaviour was possibly the most important thing of all to Hardy. In his novels, this meets with two other strands of his concern: the landscape of the countryside and the fact that all human endeavours must take place against a background of the non-human. Hardy considers human individuals against the varied and beautiful countryside that forms their environment and provides their opportunities for work and for all that they can accomplish by way of self-fulfilment. In all of this, Hardy's belief in the importance of the individual is crucial—it even has a curious stabilising effect on his political views and his personal preferences. It is a belief to which he is unfailingly loyal.

The individual personalities of the Dorset working folk he describes slide gently and permanently into the mind of the reader of the Wessex novels. Hardy can tell us in his non-fiction that working people may be witty or foolish, or analyse the states in which a labourer with a growing family may find himself, and it is all factually correct; but it is the sort of information that the he may well simply file away mentally for reference. It is harder to forget the comment on family life in *Under the Greenwood Tree*, when Fancy has gone to put on her going-away bonnet and the members of the wedding are gossiping:

' "I tell ye, naibours, when the pinch comes," said the tranter: "when the oldest daughter's boots be only a size less than her mother's, and the rest o' the flock close behind her. A sharp time for a man that, my sonnies; a very sharp time! Chanticleer's comb is a-cut then, 'a b'lieve." '

It is in the nature of fiction to be more memorable and more immediate than fact. Marty South's shorn head in *The Woodlanders* remains far more vividly in the mind than the fact that false human hair was a Victorian aid to beauty. One remembers Michael Henchard in *The Mayor of Casterbridge* with his rush basket on his back before he makes his fortune, and again after he loses it; one remembers his rages, his injustice, his remorse, as he turns from a man with 'a leonine way' and 'tigerish affection' into 'a netted lion'. Memorable, too, are Joseph Poorgrass in *Far from the Madding Crowd*, who regrets his

The hurdle-maker of Cranborne Chase. This sketch shows some of the stages in the making of a hurdle. The hurdle-maker uses a wooden plank with a row of holes bored in it. He puts hazel stems upright in the holes and then literally weaves the hurdle with split stems, with nothing else to hold them together—no nails or screws or string.

deplorable self and never forgets that '…'tis a happy providence that I be no worse, and I feel the blessing,' and Tess Durbeyfield, who instructs her little brother that human troubles probably arose because the earth was 'a blighted star'. Hardy expressed his belief in the uniqueness of individuals by inventing individuals who were unique.

He also had other lessons for the townspeople. The occasional visitor to the countryside, even if he accepted that country folk had lives, opinions and

Two pictures of a pair of working carthorses which I found at a fair near Shaftesbury. For the sepia picture, I deliberately left out the plough behind them, because I felt that the subject has been seen so often (and for good reason, as it is a delightful sight). It seemed right to paint the horses just resting there.

characters of their own, was apt to enjoy the impression each time he came that all was pretty much as it had been the last time. He could still see the farm, the farmyard, the sheep, the dairy, the cottage with its pigsty, the shepherd, the milkmaid, and the hay-trusser in the field. The scenery was indeed much the same, but the characters often were not. The second false assumption that Hardy corrected was that country people were rooted to the soil. In fact, labour was becoming increasingly mobile during the span of

A group of workers on the farm in the Marshwood Vale in the early part of November when they were using their old thrashing machine. The whole atmosphere was very happy and contented, very different from the usual sight of a lone farm-worker with earphones on, driving a tractor on a field a mile square. As these farmworkers had an attitude towards work that seemed to belong to the past, it was appropriate to include them all in a picture like a Victorian group portrait.

Hardy's attention, which reached back to the time that his grandparents could remember. Here, Hardy's great loyalty to the individual works as a counter-balance to his natural feelings of regret that some aspects of traditional life were being destroyed by the mobility of the rural population. Hardy is invariably in favour of an individual's right to move, even if this involves so many people seeking to better themselves that the good things in the old way of life are irretrievably broken up and scattered.

But he is always genuinely sorry when movement is not from choice—old Richard Broadford's eviction in *An Indiscretion in the Life of an Heiress* is

Thrashing the corn on the farm in the Marshwood Vale. It was late afternoon, and, with the sun right behind the thrashing machine, you could make out little more than the outlines of the workmen with their pitchforks and the terrier ratting.

treated with all the pity that is fitting for an individual's grief, and so is Giles Winterborne's double trouble in *The Woodlanders*, which is charcoaled on his wall by Marty South:

> 'O, Giles, you've lost your dwelling-place
> And therefore, Giles, you'll lose your Grace.'

But there is surprisingly little resentment at the underlying reason for these upsets in view of the loss of stable values that they lead to. Hardy takes the rough with the smooth, just as he expects his characters to do; he knows that privileges seldom come without obligations. If there were more security of tenure for farm labourers, this would probably accompany a condition among them approaching serfdom. Times when every man sticks to his master like a limpet are likely to be times when jobs are scarce and wages are low. The society that offers the individual the freedom to do his best for himself is the one that on balance Hardy chooses, with his eyes open to what is lost in the process.

Hardy often shows a person in adversity choosing not to move very far, but to stay close by, turning his hand to humbler work than he has been used to, employing his skills in a menial capacity so that he can stay in the countryside he likes or close to the people he loves. Henchard circling Casterbridge, a hay-trusser once more, but still not quite losing the possibility of contact with Elizabeth-Jane, or Giles Winterborne travelling the countryside from orchard to orchard making cider until he encounters Grace ('...he looked and smelt

The farmhouse in the Marshwood Vale with cabbages and the remains of bean sticks in the front garden and a little wind wafting the smoke away from the chimney. I looked back at it as I left in the evening, and it was the warm light in the window that made me want to paint it: the sort of house I would expect a farmer to live in—very simple and not at all grand or baronial. It reminded me of Shepherd Fennel's cottage in Hardy's story *The Three Strangers*.

like Autumn's very brother...'), have a good deal more to be said for them than Angel Clare, who escapes to Brazil from his perplexities, but not more than Tess, who moves to an unknown part of the countryside to be where the work is:

'Not quite sure of her direction Tess stood still upon the hemmed expanse of verdant flatness, like a fly upon a billiard-table of indefinite length, and of no more consequence to the surroundings than that fly. The sole effect of her presence upon the placid valley so far had been to excite the mind of a solitary heron, which, after descending to the ground not far from her path, stood with neck erect, looking at her.

'Suddenly there arose from all parts of the lowland a prolonged and repeated call—

An old cider orchard near Powerstock, with the cattle that are taken down through the village each day to graze there.

Right:
Cattle in a meadow near Stinsford Church. They are cross-breeds with a lot of Hereford in them.

94

' "Waow! waow! waow!"

'From the furthest east to the furthest west the cries spread as if by contagion, accompanied in some cases by the barking of a dog. It was not the expression of the valley's consciousness that beautiful Tess had arrived, but the ordinary announcement of milking-time—half-past four o' clock, when the dairymen set about getting in the cows.

'The red and white herd nearest at hand, which had been phlegmatically waiting for the call, now trooped towards the steading in the background, their great bags of milk swinging under them as they walked. Tess followed slowly in their rear, and entered the barton by the open gate through which they had entered before her. Long thatched sheds stretched round the

The watermeadows of the Frome Valley. The fence goes out into the river at the bend to provide a place where the cattle can drink and stops them wandering off along the river.

enclosure, their slopes encrusted with vivid green moss, and their eaves supported by wooden posts rubbed to a glossy smoothness by the flanks of infinite cows and calves of bygone years…'

As Tess joins the group of dairy workers, she gets more of a welcome than she might have done:

'The majority of dairymen have a cross manner at milking-time, but it happened that Mr Crick was glad to get a new hand—for the days were busy ones now—and he received her warmly…'

Lucky Tess. A longish journey to a strange place has not ended as badly as it might have done. Soon she will meet Angel Clare, '…daily, in that strange and solemn interval, the twilight of the morning, in the violet or pink dawn…'

Near Tincleton. Cattle grazing in the Frome Valley in the cool clean light of early spring with everything softened by a misty morning haze. This is a scene I associate with Tess as a milkmaid—perhaps the best time of her life. The only difference is that the cattle are Friesians, which they would not have been in Tess's day, but I have, of course, painted everything as it is in the 1980s.

and all summer long enjoy 'Another year's instalment of flowers, leaves, nightingales, thrushes, finches and such ephemeral creatures...' and the waterfowl that they can see from the moist meadows. Tess '...possibly never would be so happy again.'

She had come a long way for her happiness. To the visitor, it would be apparent that there was a milkmaid at work, just as there had been the previous summer. And so there was, but it was a different milkmaid. The countryside was no static pastoral scene; it was rippling with the movement of people.

The people of the countryside were also socially mobile: Tess's father's belief that he was descended from the nobility was not so very unusual. There were many such stories, and some of them were true:

'Why, our little Retty Priddle here, you know, is one of the Paridelles—the old family that used to own lots o' the lands out by King's-Hintock now owned by the Earl o' Wessex...'

Among the reasons for mobility in the countryside were the laws and customs that governed the ownership and tenancy of homes. The need to find a new home might arise from the falling-in of a lease—occupants whose tenancies ended with the death of one of their number or with the death of a nearby tenant could find themselves homeless after a long tenure. Tenants of a farmer, who might himself be a tenant, could be evicted to suit his changing needs; worst at risk were '...the unattached labourers, approximating to the free labourers of the middle ages, who are to be found in the larger villages and small towns of the county—many of them, no doubt, descendants of the old copyholders who were ousted from their little plots when the system of leasing large farms grew general.'

Copyholders had something closer to security of tenure, as their occupation was at the pleasure of the manor landlord, not the tenant farmer. 'Copyholders, cottage freeholders and the like,' Hardy noted, 'are as a rule less trim and neat, more muddling in their ways, than the dependent labourer; and yet there is no more comfortable or serene being than the cottager who is sure of his roof.' But security of tenure had become less common than it was. Hardy reviews the advantages of permanent and close association with a district that this security had lent the workfolk, but he describes the former state of affairs all the same as '...the centuries of serfdom, of copyholding tenants...'

Now, increasingly, 'The landlord does not know by sight, if even by name, half the men who preserve his acres from the curse of Eden. They come and go yearly, like birds of passage, nobody thinks whence or whither. This dissociation is favoured by the customary system of letting the cottage with the land, so that, far from having a guarantee of a holding to keep him fixed, the labourer has not even the stability of a landlord's tenant; he is only tenant

Blackbird and songthrush—two species of bird that Hardy would have been able to see as he sat in his study at Max Gate, where he wrote his poem *Birds at Winter Nightfall*.

of a tenant, the latter possibly a new comer, who takes strictly commercial views of his man and cannot afford to waste a penny on sentimental consider-ations.' The change has a disadvantageous effect on the traditions of a district and on the labourers' intimate knowledge of its geography and special features, and a very disruptive effect on the schooling of the children con-cerned; more and more tradesmen of the better sort, who used to be a mainstay of village life, pack up and go to the towns, to the detriment of the village concerned and without improving their own quality of life. But for the majority, the labourers themselves, the sometimes yearly moves are pleasant adventures; on Lady Day, Old Style, 6th April, the carter of the new em-ployer is sent to collect the incoming workman and his family:

The farm near Corfe Castle with its traditional farmyard. The farmhouse and barn are both built of stone, and the barn is thatched. There was no concrete anywhere, just packed earth and gravel in which the chickens were scratching around. I have painted it exactly as I saw it and not romanticised it at all.
Right:
The farmer just stood watching me as I worked. One of his cows was standing behind him—at one stage it came and licked his ear and the back of his jacket. The cow had horns and the dog was the sort of farmyard dog you hardly see today, a cross-breed with some bearded collie in it—the sort of dog that the old shepherds might have had.

'The goods are built up on the waggon to a well-nigh unvarying pattern, which is probably as peculiar to the country labourer as the hexagon to the bee. The dresser, with its finger-marks and domestic evidences thick upon it, stands importantly in front... The hive of bees is slung up to the axle of the waggon, and alongside it the cooking pot or crock, within which are stowed the roots of garden flowers. Barrels are largely used for crockery, and budding gooseberry bushes are suspended by the roots; while on the top of the furniture a circular nest is made of the bed and bedding for the matron and children, who sit there through the journey...

I was searching Toller Down for scenes that reminded me of Gabriel Oak in *Far from the Madding Crowd*, when I turned a corner in the track to see this flock of sheep being driven up towards me.

'The day of removal, if fine, wears an aspect of jollity, and the whole proceeding is a blithe one.'

The need to move might come from misfortune or eviction, but enterprise or ambition might bring about the same train of events—the hiring fair, new employment, a piled wagon. A labourer who felt that his work was unappreciated or his future insecure, or that his growing family were turning from mouths to be fed into employable assets, could simply take his household to

On the Dorset downland: the broken-down remains of a hut in which a shepherd would have lived at lambing time.

more prosperous pastures. When skilled men were in demand, they could often improve their conditions of service by being prepared to leave in search of better; if disaster struck, there were more places than one where livings could be sought.

Gabriel Oak, in *Far from the Madding Crowd*, has built up an economically viable flock of two hundred and fifty ewes when an over-enthusiastic young sheepdog drives this treasure over a cliff:

'The sheep were not insured. All the savings of a frugal life had been dispersed at a blow; his hopes of being an independent farmer were laid low—

Sheep on the downland between West Milton and Powerstock, looking across to what is left of the ancient field system of strip lynchets.

104

possibly for ever… Stupors, however, do not last for ever, and Farmer Oak recovered from his.'

He does the sensible thing and goes to the February hiring fair at Casterbridge:

'In the crowd was an athletic young fellow of somewhat superior appearance to the rest—in fact his superiority was marked enough to lead several ruddy peasants standing by to speak to him inquiringly, as to a farmer, and to use 'Sir' as a finishing word. His answer always was,—

Dorset Horn sheep, which Hardy would have seen when he was thinking about the character of Gabriel Oak. Quite a few flocks remain, although they are no longer the predominant breed in Dorset.

A Dorset owl which was given to me by an antique dealer friend. It is a round earthenware container with a glazed top which farmworkers would have carried into the harvest field with cider or ale in it. The holes are to take a string or a leather strap for carrying. The pottery is very thick to keep the contents cool.

' "I am looking for a place myself—a bailiff's. Do ye know of anybody who wants one?" '

Gabriel is not offered a post as a bailiff at Casterbridge Fair, nor yet as a shepherd. He plays with the idea that he should have listened to the blandishments of the recruiting sergeant—that last resort. But on his way to Shotsford Fair, he proves himself a useful man at dealing with a rick fire, and he encounters his lost love, Bathsheba—his future wife. She has inherited a farm of her own—her fortunes have gone up by chance, just as his have gone down. Both recognise the difference that it makes, but among their mixed feelings, embarrassment is not included. It is 'not without gallantry' that Gabriel accosts her: 'Do you happen to want a shepherd, ma'am?' Their long working association is from choice. Bathsheba dismisses Gabriel because she chooses to, and when she begs him to come back, he does so because he chooses to. When he finally wins his 'skittish Bathsheba', she shares with him the prosperity that he has helped to build. He has by then experienced many of the fluctuations in fortune that the countryside can provide for a man who is determined to earn his living from it. Some of them are beyond his control, many can be survived by hard work. And everything can be ruined by bad luck. Gabriel Oak may lose a flock, or win a farm. Michael Henchard may make and lose a fortune in a lifetime. Milkmaids, shepherds, labourers and prosperous farmers are always to be seen in the countryside, but they sometimes change places.

Other forces may operate against the even tenor of a settled existence on the land and even against the desire for it. One of these is education. Grace, in *The Woodlanders*, who has a devoted father and a happy future as a woodlander's wife planned out for her, is all but ruined by it. She has been educated out of her class and has chosen badly from the limited number of specimens at her disposal in the class above. Extreme lack of education can be as bad. Tess suffers from this deprivation: a very small amount of guidance might have saved her from Alec D'Urberville, but the hints on life and her prospects that she received at home have driven her into his arms.

An unsatisfied craving for real education— the acquisition of knowledge and wisdom, with rising in the world a mere side effect—can be an excruciating torment, as Jude discovers. He and Sue flirt with ideas, amazed at them, sometimes terrified by them, but are unwelcome in the world in which they would be better able to assimilate them. The hunger for knowledge could be hard on those of the uneducated who knew enough to know that they were excluded from its haunts.

Perhaps only Clym in *The Return of the Native* has the right ideas about education and the countryside—he has had an education and, having assimilated it, wants only to use it for the good of simple people, to help them make their lives richer and lighter. Misfortune overtakes him and weakens his potential authority. His end as 'an itinerant open-air preacher and lecturer on morally unimpeachable subjects...' is a compromise, but one that is good enough for him and perhaps good enough for Hardy. For the rest, when Clym preached:

'Some believed him, and some believed not; some said that his words were commonplace, others complained of his want of theological doctrine; while others again remarked that it was well enough for a man to take to preaching who could not see to do anything else.'

Clym's way of life as an itinerant preacher is an instance of another element that can raise itself against the claims of home and hearth and a settled

I met a group of gipsies near Shaftesbury at the time of a big local fair. The girls echoed the last century in their appearance and clothing, and some of the others were sitting and making pegs. There can now only be a handful of families who travel around entirely in horse-drawn vehicles as they do. I wish I had been able to do more with the subject, but although I looked for the gipsies again, I was never able to find them.

existence, even where these can be reasonably easily achieved. And it was an aspect that was even less understood by townspeople than the agricultural life. Londoners tended to think that any wandering about the countryside was done by gipsies. In reality, a wide range of occupations depended on an itinerant life. Clym took to it because he had found a vocation.

In the same novel, Diggory Venn takes up the trade of travelling reddleman because it suits him. He is sad not to be married to his dear Thomasin, he wants a change and to keep a regular eye on the district. He is not wasting his time—his expenses are small and his extraordinary occupation profitable. He terrifies the neighbourhood children because his ware, a marking dye for sheep, saturates his hair and hands and face with its monstrous redness, but he knows that it will wash off in the end. He is a traveller from choice. So, too,

Left:
At a small agricultural show at Bridport, I was looking at the heavy horses when I saw this wonderful Shire horse being shown off by his handler to a couple of other people. The horse, however, was more interested in a mare that was moving around behind the two men.

Farmyard buildings.

Overleaf:
The porch of Puddletown Church which corresponds to the one where Troy slept in *Far from the Madding Crowd*.

are the gipsies, or the strolling players who offer entertainment at Caster-bridge, or the showmen at fairs, or the furmity woman who so strangely affects Michael Henchard's life, or Henchard himself, when as a young man and again as an old one, he seeks work as a hay-trusser wherever he can find it. They are not great travellers or adventurers, like those who seek farms and fortunes overseas or march off, as John Loveday does in *The Trumpet Major*, to 'blow his trumpet till silenced for ever upon one of the bloody battle-fields of Spain.' These itinerant workers were country-dwellers, and showed that there was more to the countryside than a familiar cottage door—more flexibility, more ways of life that could accommodate a person than the town knew about, and these were not always chosen from necessity. The charlatan doctor who plies his trade from place to place and does Jude little good and Arabella only slightly more, travelling musicians, Giles Winterborne comp-etently making cider round the counties, the hangman who comes and goes: these are men who have found a place in the countryside, just as much as the settled miller or stone-mason, tranter or turner.

Hardy is full of pity when people are driven out of the countryside com-pletely. 'Villages used to contain,' he says, 'in addition to the agricultural inhabitants, an interesting and better-informed class, ranking distinctly above those—the blacksmith, the carpenter, the shoemaker, the small higgler, the shopkeeper...' As their life holdings fell in, landlords generally declined to grant further tenancies, but instead pulled down any cottages that they did not need to house their own labourers. The families had to move, to 'seek refuge in the boroughs. This process, which is designated by the statisticians as "the tendency of the rural population towards the large towns," is really the tendency of water to flow uphill when forced.'

V
TOWNS

When they are not forced to use towns as a last resort, country-dwellers look at them rather in the way that town-dwellers look at the countryside—as extraneous, almost accidentally available, not quite part of real life, into which they make occasional forays before quickly returning home.

Hardy's own attitude to towns was that of an intelligent countryman. He was deeply sorry for the trapped inhabitants of the capital. 'London. Four million lost hopes!' was a journal entry for 1889. However, London contained things he needed. It was where publishers, critics and other writers were to be found; there were church services with splendid music, art exhibitions, dinner

Bridport, which appears as Port Bredy in a couple of Hardy's stories. As I did not want to draw cars, I went to the towns very early in the morning, before anyone was up. Although my subject was the architecture, I left the traffic lights in because it would have falsified the picture of Bridport now to remove them.

parties, praise, recognition, understanding and, initially, good advice. From the real environment of the countryside, he made his sorties and returned unscathed.

This is also the way in which towns are normally used by his right-minded country-dwelling characters, such as Lady Constantine in *Two on a Tower*:

'In the days of her prosperity Lady Constantine had often gone to the city of Bath, either frivolously, for shopping purposes, or musico-religiously, to attend choir festivals in the abbey...'

Later, penurious and in love, she goes to Bath to achieve her objective of a private wedding. Even on this economical and practical visit, she sensibly uses a walk in the aisles of the abbey to calm her nerves. She does some minor shopping as well.

Woolbridge House, and Wool Bridge over the Frome, both of them Elizabethan. Woolbridge House is the original of Wellbridge House, where Tess and Angel Clare spent their wedding night in *Tess of the D'Urbervilles*.

Eustacia, in *The Return of the Native*, longs for Budmouth (Weymouth) nearly as much as she longs for Paris. Eustacia's descents on people or places are all-or-nothing affairs. She does not want to go to Budmouth in a sensible manner, to get what she wants and come away; she simply wants the freedom of the place, and when she is told that she can have it, but in exchange for light work, the idea is spoiled for her.

She would have jumped at the fate that Tess so hated. Tess had very little use for towns, but was taken by Alec D'Urberville to live in Sandbourne (Bournemouth) as his mistress:

'This fashionable watering-place, with its eastern and western stations, its piers, its groves of pines, its promenades, and its covered gardens, was, to Angel Clare, like a fairy place suddenly created by the stroke of a wand, and allowed to get a little dusty.'

Tess and Angel escape into the countryside like salmon up-river. Sandbourne represents nearly all Tess's experience of towns, although she is taken to Wintoncester (Winchester) to be hanged.

For Jude, towns hold many things that he wants. He tries to use towns in the right way, to acquire the things that they seem to offer—help with his education and work to support his family while he improves himself. But Christminster (Oxford) snubs him. He is conscious of a link with the dead craftsmen who built the amazing colleges, but when he sits down, prepared to love the city, a policeman moves him on from his plinth-stone. The master of Biblioll College advises him to be content with his life as a working man.

Melchester (Salisbury), however, is 'a quiet, soothing place, almost entirely ecclesiastical in its tone; a spot where worldly learning and intellectual smartness had no establishment; where the altruistic feeling that he did possess would perhaps be more highly estimated than a brilliancy which he did not.' Jude fancies that here he will be able to work at his trade and to absorb theology in its proper setting. With Sue, he begins to taste town life a little—the park, the castle, picture galleries, the cathedral service. But when she marries:

'He could no longer endure the light of the Melchester lamps; the sunshine was as drab paint; and the blue sky as zinc.'

Jude pursues Sue to Shaston (Shaftesbury), and finds that although 'Shaston, the ancient British Palladour…was, and is, in itself the city of a dream', it is nothing to him, except as Sue's married home. In Aldbrickham (Reading), with Sue beside him, Jude renews his attempts to benefit from the riches of the towns, to avail himself of the knowledge and the livelihoods to be found there. He does manage to go to a public lecture and to get some low-paid work as a stonemason. But because of the couple's history, Sue's views on

The road to Shaftesbury (Shaston), the outskirts of which can be seen up on the skyline at the right of the picture. I am particularly attached to Shaftesbury as it is the place where I found my first shepherd's crook.

marriage and their general lack of information as to how the world works, she is soon saying, 'We mustn't go to Alfredston, or to Melchester, or to Shaston, or to Christminster. Apart from those we may go anywhere.' Hardy had thought of calling the book, not *Jude the Obscure*, but *The Simpletons*.

Jude and Sue are reduced to seeking from towns the one thing they always provide for a while: the chance to live among strangers. Jude is not strong enough to succeed in his attempts to extract what he wants out of the towns. Indeed, to think of assailing them for their special goods—their classical education, their theological doctrine, their money-making, their architectural glories—is a truly formidable task, one that is within Hardy's powers, but not within Jude's. Towns, for Jude, are sometimes forests to hide in, and sometimes fortresses, unassailable in their self-sufficiency and self-assurance—the

117

outsider should think twice before throwing himself on their sparse hospitality and generosity. To stay in them, a person almost needs a passport, friends at court and a handbook of the laws.

London itself is well outside Wessex, while Christminster is near Wessex's northern border. Jude's towns, Aldbrickham and elsewhere, are in the north, not the heart of Wessex. Melchester and Shaston are closer to this heart, but Melchester is remote because of its religious atmosphere, and beautiful Shaston is somehow separate, up on its hill. The town at the heart of Hardy's country is Casterbridge, which is a model of what a town should be, 'as compact as a box of dominoes...'

'To birds of the more soaring kind Casterbridge must have appeared on this fine evening as a mosaic-work of subdued reds, browns, greys, and crystals, held together by a rectangular frame of deep green...

'The lamp lights now glimmered through the engirdling trees, conveying a sense of great snugness and comfort inside, and rendering at the same time the unlighted country without strangely solitary and vacant in aspect, considering its nearness to life.'

A town close to the country, easily distinguishable from it, offering comfort, even friendliness to human beings, for natural reciprocal reasons:

'The agricultural and pastoral character of the people upon whom the town depended for its existence was shown by the class of objects displayed in the shop windows. Scythes, reap-hooks, sheep-shears, bill-hooks, spades, mattocks, and hoes at the ironmonger's; bee-hives, butter-firkins, churns, milking stools and pails, hay-rakes, field flagons, and seed-lips at the cooper's; cart-ropes and plough-harness at the saddler's; carts, wheel-barrows and millgear at the wheel-wright's and machinist's; horse embrocation at the chemist's; at the glover's and leather-cutter's, hedging gloves, thatchers' knee-caps, plough-men's leggings, villagers' pattens and clogs.'

This is a town of properly human dimensions, depending, and knowing that it depends, on the countryside it serves, a town with good inns, good churches, chiming clocks, tolling bells, a curfew that shopkeepers find useful as a signal to close their shutters, a jail and an almshouse, a past stretching back to pre-Roman times, and a market where real money is exchanged for real goods. It is a town that has never taken off from its true beginnings into one of the exotic, other-worldly variations that take so much courage to approach and are so stony to the stranger, but has remained in its proper relation to the surrounding corn-lands:

'Casterbridge...was a place deposited in the block upon a corn-field. There was no suburb in the modern sense, or transitional intermixture of town and

Dorchester—Hardy's home town, which is called Casterbridge in his novels. This view looks straight down the main street.

`Left:
Shepherd's crooks and sheep bells, all from Dorset. They were bought from the widow of a shepherd who worked in the area of Shaftesbury and Gillingham.

down. It stood, with regard to the wide fertile land adjoining, clean-cut and distinct, like a chess-board on a green tablecloth. The farmer's boy could sit under his barley-mow and pitch a stone into the office-window of the town clerk; reapers at work among the sheaves nodded to acquaintances standing on the pavement-corner; the red-robed judge, when he condemned a sheep-stealer, pronounced sentence to the tune of Baa, that floated in at the window from the remainder of the flock browsing hard by; and at executions the waiting crowd stood in a meadow immediately before the drop, out of which the cows had been temporarily driven to give the spectators room.'

The town lives 'by agriculture at one remove'. It does have a slum, called Mixen Lane, but the inhabitants slip in picturesquely from an evening's poaching by way of planks of wood thrown across a stream.

In this town, the prosperous, settled town-dweller can lead a decorous, secure sort of life:

'The front doors of the private houses were mostly left open at this warm autumn time, no thought of umbrella stealers disturbing the minds of the placid burgesses. Hence, through the long straight entrance passages thus unclosed could be seen, as through tunnels, the mossy gardens at the back, glowing with nasturtiums, fuchsias, scarlet geraniums, "bloody warriors", snapdragons, and dahlias, this floral blaze being backed by crusted grey stonework remaining from a yet remoter Casterbridge than the venerable one visible in the street.'

A country person could well live in a town like this without losing his bearings: the town has not lost its links with the countryside, which is only a step away. Even as a boy, Hardy had never found the distance from Higher Bockhampton to Dorchester very daunting.

The King's Arms Hotel, one of the old inns of Dorchester.

VI

TOWN AND COUNTRY

The hero of *Jude the Obscure* is called Jude Fawley, after the meagre village of Great Fawley in the north of Wessex, where Hardy's grandmother had been born. This might suggest an element of autobiography, but the novel is actually a work of the horrified imagination. Jude was no Thomas Hardy, but it is hard to believe that his creation did not spring from that little shudder familiar to people for whom things have gone reasonably well, when they consider how, but for the grace of God, things might have gone: the wasted

Bullfinches, simply because Hardy wrote a poem called *The Bullfinches*.

122

hopes, the unsuccessful forays into the towns and cities, the return to the countryside never accomplished. Hardy achieved in towns what Jude did not: he managed to extract from them exactly what he needed.

In towns, he always indulged his love for built things. Hardy, the architect turned novelist, loved to look at good, expensively wrought buildings, and, in particular, at churches. His enthusiasm was increasingly that of an onlooker.

One of the many ancient drove ways that cut across the face of Dorset, often sunk down between steep banks. These are places in which you are very likely to see a fox. This one was crossing the path and momentarily turned its head towards me before disappearing.

A gateway in a village in the Marshwood Vale.

It generally did not take him long to turn from the thing built to the builder and to the sense of the past preserved in the present. *The Abbey Mason* is a cheerful ballad about a mason who solves an architectural problem by studying patterns of icicles when worry stops him sleeping: he realises what God has created in Nature and accidentally invents the Perpendicular Gothic style:

Right:
Details of cottages in the same village. The owner of one wanted to move her dustbin out of the way while I painted her back door, but I wanted it left there. In the other cottage, I liked the bean sticks, and the loganberries that were growing round the window. The lady who was picking them at the time ran away and hid because she did not want me to include her in the picture.

—Well, when in Wessex on your rounds,
Take a brief step beyond its bounds,

And enter Gloucester: seek the quoin
Where choir and transept interjoin,

And gazing at the forms there flung
Against the sky by one unsung—

The ogee arches transom-topped,
The tracery stalks by spandrels stopped,

Petrified lacework—lightly lined
On ancient massiveness behind—

Muse that some minds so modest be
As to renounce fame's fairest fee,

(Like him who crystallized on this spot
His visionings, but lies forgot,

And many a medieval one
Whose symmetries salute the sun) ...

Hardy enjoyed looking with an architect's eye. He knew that detail was important in one way and structure in another, and that, while either was being worked on, someone had to be in charge of overseeing the whole thing—someone lively minded and observant, who could, like the Abbey Mason, do

'...but what all artists do,
Wait upon Nature for his cue...'

Over and above the satisfaction and stimulus he could find in appreciating buildings, London provided Hardy with the chance to know the work of artists, who, if he had stayed in the country, might have remained unfamiliar to him. The work of J.M.W. Turner was particularly important to him, not just for the pleasure he could derive from it, but because it reassured him that he was right to express deep and turbulent thoughts. He had always been taught and permitted self-expression. From his childhood in the village, he knew that music-making was enjoyable and respected as an accomplishment when it was subordinated to the needs of Christmas frolics or a local wedding; he knew from his student life and his professional career that the knowledge and skills needed to restore a church were good to possess and useful to society. But he suspected that there might be more to the arts than this, and it was a relief when he was sure of it. He wrote in 1887:

A nightingale in Cranborne Chase. This was in May, when the ground was carpeted with bluebells.

126

'The "simply natural" is interesting no longer. The much decried, mad, late-Turner rendering is now necessary to create my interest. The exact truth as to material fact ceases to be of importance in art—it is a student's style—the style of a period when the mind is serene and unawakened to the tragical mysteries of life; when it does not bring anything to the object that coalesces with and translates the qualities that are already there,—half-hidden, it may be—and the two united are depicted as the All.'

And, after a concert in 1906, he commented:

'I prefer late Wagner, as I prefer late Turner... today it was early Wagner for the most part: fine music, but not so particularly his—no spectacle of the inside of a brain at work like the inside of a hive.'

Turner and Wagner helped Hardy to put his mind at rest about himself. Music continued to be important to him. He wrote of Michael Henchard, the mayor

Sheep tucked under a hedge.

A Dorset gate, with steel rods and a wooden frame, which is quite different from the five-bar gates of other areas. I believe that this sort of gate is still made. The shape of the oak tree is also characteristic, particularly in parts near the sea. This was probably only four or five miles inland.

of Casterbridge, that 'If he could have summoned music to his aid, his existence might even now have been borne...' The Hardys went to plenty of concerts when they were in London. Hardy also haunted the music halls of London and Paris; in smaller towns, he went out of his way to attend circuses and fairs, for he did not intend to let solemnity colour his imagination more than seemed reasonable.

London provided many things that Hardy needed: contacts and contracts, notices, reviews, praise, the renewing of friendships. Each time he went to the capital, he equipped himself with these worldly essentials, and then returned to the countryside to live and work.

There is no doubt that most of what Hardy wanted was in the country, and that, cut off from it, he would have shrivelled up for lack of nourishment, just

as, if he had stayed all his life in the country, he would have become baffled and discouraged by the difference between his own capacity for feeling and expression and what was required along these lines by his neighbours. Neither shrivelled nor baffled, he returned home.

In the country, he sometimes considered his own end, just as Tess had done:

Virtually at twilight, looking out from the top of Eggardon Hill toward Golden Cap and the sea, which can just be glimpsed on the skyline, shimmering with the last rays of the sun. You can see a little of the switchback coastline of Dorset, bathed in golden light over Golden Cap, with the dark coombes and valleys in the foreground.

'She suddenly thought one afternoon, when looking in the glass at her fairness, that there was yet another date, of greater importance to her than those; that of her own death, when all these charms would have disappeared; a day which lay sly and unseen among all the other days of the year, giving no sign or sound when she annually passed over it; but not the less surely there.' She had Jeremy Taylor's thought that some time in the future those who had known her would say: ' "It is the —th, the day that poor Tess Durbeyfield died"; and there would be nothing singular to their minds in the statement.'

When Hardy thought the matter through for himself, he took great care in choosing what he would like to have associated with his memory. He listed the results in *Afterwards*:

130

When the Present has latched its postern behind my tremulous stay,
　　And the May month flaps its glad green leaves like wings,
Delicate-filmed as new spun silk, will the neighbours say,
　　"He was a man who used to notice such things"?

If it be in the dusk when, like an eyelid's soundless blink,
　　The dewfall-hawk comes crossing the shades to alight
Upon the wind-warped upland thorn, a gazer may think,
　　"To him this must have been a familiar sight."

If I pass during some nocturnal blackness, mothy and warm,
　　When the hedgehog travels furtively over the lawn,
One may say, "He strove that such innocent creatures should come to no harm
　　But he could do little for them; and now he is gone."

If, when hearing that I have been stilled at last, they stand at the door,
　　Watching the full-starred heavens that winter sees,
Will this thought rise on those who will meet my face no more,
　　"He was one who had an eye for such mysteries"?

And will any say when my bell of quittance is heard in the gloom,
　　And a crossing breeze cuts a pause in its outrollings,
Till they rise again, as they were a new bell's boom
　　"He hears it not now, but used to notice such things?"

Above all, Hardy wanted to be remembered as a man who noticed. The objects of his attention, the things he loved were all from the natural world of the countryside. It is as if he had collected and stored up images as a small boy lying in the grass looking around him, and then recalled them to use in his writing. None of these images is very dramatically portrayed. *Afterwards* reads like a fastidious, muted claim to have appreciated to the full a few 'neutral-tinted haps'.

But it is, nevertheless, an enormous claim. To have understood and have been close to the seasons and the times of day, to the landscape, to small animals in their habitats, to the stars, whose names he had known so long, to the sound of church bells, and to neighbours: this is a major boast to make about a life.

And, if anyone cared to examine Hardy's claims, they would stand up to inspection. Hardy had consistently liked and honoured all these things, and his work is there to prove it.

The view from the grass was there in *The Return of the Native*:

'At length she reached a slope about two-thirds of the whole distance from Alderworth to her own home, where a little patch of shepherd's-thyme intruded on the path; and she sat down upon the perfumed mat it formed there. In front of her a colony of ants had established a thoroughfare across the way, where they toiled, a never-ending and heavy-laden throng... She leant back to obtain more thorough rest, and the soft eastern portion of the sky was as great a relief to her eyes as the thyme was to her head. While she looked a heron arose on that side of the sky and flew on with his face towards the sun. He had come dripping wet from some pool in the valleys, and as he flew the edges and linings of his wings, his thighs, and his breast were so caught by the bright sunbeams that he appeared as if formed of burnished silver.'

The open downland of Eggardon Hill, an early British hill fort, which is ridged from centuries of grazing by sheep.

132

Eggardon Hill at night, with the road running across the ramparts. I was up on top of Eggardon a couple of years back with a friend looking for ghosts; we didn't find any, although we did see some glow-worms.

The stars had been out in *Far from the Madding Crowd*:

'The sky was clear—remarkably clear—and the twinkling of all the stars seemed to be but throbs of one body, timed by a common pulse. The North Star was directly in the wind's eye, and since evening the Bear had swung round it outwardly to the east, till he was now at a right angle with the meridian. A difference of colour in the stars—oftener read of than seen in England—was really perceptible here. The kingly brilliancy of Sirius pierced the eye with a steely glitter, the star called Capella was yellow, Aldebaran and Betelgueux shone with a fiery red.

'To persons standing on a hill during a clear midnight such as this, the roll of the world eastward is almost a palpable movement.'

The seasons mingled with the activities of the characters in *The Woodlanders*, and all but the worst of these characters shared Hardy's pleasure in the changing year:

'The breakfast hour went by heavily enough, and the next followed in the same, half-snowy, half-rainy style, the weather now being the inevitable relapse which sooner or later succeeds a time too radiant for the season, such as they had enjoyed in the late mid-winter at Hintock. To people at home there these changeful tricks had their interest; the strange mistakes that some of the more sanguine trees had made in budding before their month, to be incontinently glued up by frozen thawings now; the similar sanguine errors of impulsive birds in framing nests that were swamped by snow-water, and other

The pathway that leads along the banks of the Frome from Lower Bockhampton to Stinsford Church. It was one of Hardy's favourite walks, a very fresh, green place, with moorhens and other water birds. It is very enclosed, with hedgerows and trees beside the path, all the way to the church. I like the inviting feeling of the path that makes you want to walk through and out into the sunlight.

The watermeadows of the Frome Valley in summer.

such incidents, prevented any sense of wearisomeness in the minds of the natives. But these were features of a world not familiar to Fitzpiers, and the inner visions to which he had almost exclusively attended having suddenly failed in their power to absorb him, he felt unutterably dreary.'

Hardy had always been a close observer of the natural world, but he also noticed the 'worn threshold' implying human habitation, which was sometimes even more thought-provoking than nature itself, and found inspiration

135

in the people of the countryside, who could be good, bad, disappointed, cheerful or simply funny.

When Hardy wrote *Afterwards* at Max Gate, he was only a short distance from his birthplace, and he felt that he was near the end of his life, a life in which he had explored the roads that had stretched out before him as a child—to Casterbridge, Shaston, Melchester, Aldbrickham, London, Lyonesse. It was in the valley of the Frome, with its lush watermeadows, its wind-warped heath, its market town and its human and animal inhabitants going about their business, that he found the sensible centre of the universe, the place to which he always returned.

The Frome Valley.

AT DAY-CLOSE IN NOVEMBER

The ten hours' light is abating,
    And a late bird wings across,
Where the pines, like waltzers waiting,
    Give their black heads a toss.

Beech leaves, that yellow the noon-time,
    Float past like specks in the eye;
I set every tree in my June time,
    And now they obscure the sky.

And the children who ramble through here
    Conceive that there never has been
A time when no tall trees grew here,
    That none will in time be seen.

INDEX